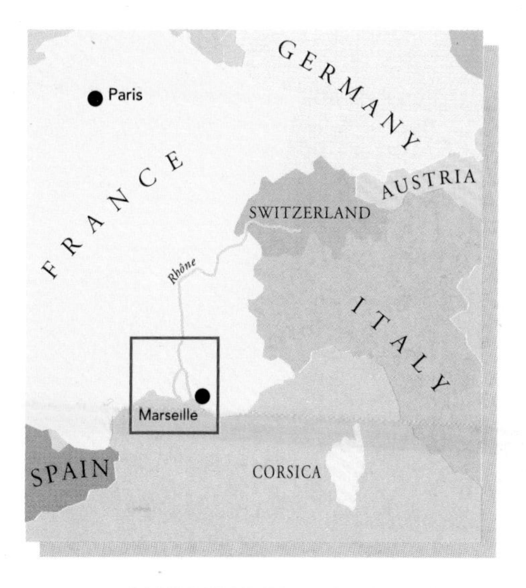

PATRICK DELAFORCE

HarperCollins*Publishers*

This book was produced using QuarkXPress™ and
Adobe Illustrator 88™ on Apple Macintosh™ computers
and output to separated film on a Linotronic™ 300 Imagesetter

Text: Patrick Delaforce
Photography: Stuart Boreham
Cartography: Susan Harvey
Design: Lynsey Roxburgh

First published 1991

Published by HarperCollins Publishers
Produced by Collins Manufacturing, Glasgow
ISBN 0 00 435850-3

HOW TO USE THIS BOOK

Your Collins Traveller Guide will help you find your way around your holiday destination quickly and easily. It is split into two sections which are colour-coded:

The blue section provides you with an alphabetical sequence of headings, from **ART GALLERIES** to **WALKS** via **EXCURSIONS**, **RESTAURANTS**, **SHOPPING**, etc. Each entry within a topic includes information on how to get there, how much it will cost you, when it will be open and what to expect. Furthermore, every page has its own map showing the position of each item and the nearest landmark. This allows you to orientate yourself quickly and easily in your new surroundings.
To find what you want to do – having dinner, visiting a museum, going for a walk or shopping for gifts – simply flick through the blue headings and take your pick!

The red section is an alphabetical list of information. It provides essential facts about places and cultural items – 'What are *santons*?', 'When is the Orange Carnival?', 'Where is Vaison-la-Romaine?' – and expands on subjects touched on in the first half of the book. This section also contains practical travel information. It ranges through how to find accommodation, where to hire a car, the variety of eating places and food available, tips on health, information on money, which newspapers are available, how to find a taxi and where the Youth Hostels are. It is lively and informative and easy to use. Each band shows the first three letters of the first entry on the page. Simply flick through the bands till you find the entry you need!

All the main entries are also cross-referenced to help you find them. Names in small capitals – **CHILDREN** – tell you that there is more information about the item you are looking for under the topic on children in the first part of the book. So when you read 'see **CHILDREN**' you turn to the blue heading for **CHILDREN**. The instruction 'see **A-Z**', after a word, lets you know that the word has its own entry in the second part of the book. Similarly words in bold type – **Arles** – also let you know that there is an entry in the gazetteer for the indicated name. In both cases you just look under the appropriate heading in the red section. Packed full of information and easy to use – you'll always know where you are with your Collins Traveller Guide!

Rhône
rue Marie Jouveau
rue de la Cavalerie
OLIVIER
Prieuré
rue du Quatre Septembre
LOU GARDIAN
rue Volta
PAILLOTTE
rue de la Calade
LE VACCARES
rue du Cloître
LOU MARQUES
rue Emile Fassin

INTRODUCTION

Provence conjures up visions of brilliant colours – the yellow cornfields, purple lavender beds and red or black mountains which inspired Van Gogh and Cézanne – sensual smells, colourful cuisine, husky wines, summer music and Roman antiquities. The daily markets in its towns and villages display luscious tomatoes, olives, peppers, aubergines, artichokes and courgettes, soon to be made into the famous *cuisine Provençale:* dishes of *bouillabaisse, ratatouille, bourride* or *daube,* flavoured with garlic, olive oil, thyme, sage and rosemary and washed down by Châteauneuf-du-Pape, Gigondas and Côtes de Provence wines from vineyards originally planted by the Greeks.

Provence also offers exciting artistic events. The long-established international music festivals in Orange and Aix-en-Provence, and theatre in Avignon attract thousands of the faithful in midsummer. But every tiny village has its summer fête and fair with folk and religious traditions: Les Saintes-Maries-de-la-Mer for the gypsies, Tarascon with its biblical 'monster', and the pastoral transhumance night of St. Jean in Valréas, are examples.

The area's ten major Roman sites include some of the wonders of the world and should not be missed, nor should the Gothic Palais des Papes at Avignon; the mysterious hillside village of the Lords of Les Baux; the Fontaine-de-Vaucluse made famous by the Italian poet Petrarch; and the ramparted town of Aigues-Mortes. Visit too the evocative Camargue, land of pink flamingoes, wild white horses, ferocious little black bulls and proud *gardien* cowboys. It is a major ornithological reserve, attracting hundreds of migrant birds.

Provence has several hundred kilometres of shore line, as well as a dozen resorts with good bathing, such as Cassis, La Ciotat and Carry-le-Rouet, plus scores of highly organized camp sites which make a holiday in the area ideal for families with children. The hinterland of the Vaucluse offers delightful walks, particularly in the Nature Park of the Lubéron and the Mount Ventoux range east of Orange and the dozens of little hillside villages such as Gordes, Sablet, Ansouis and Roussillon,

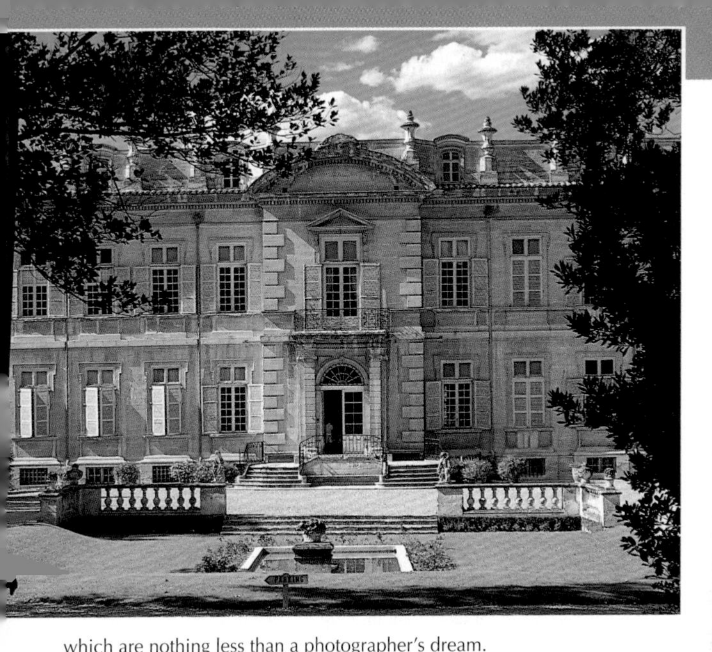

which are nothing less than a photographer's dream.
There are a few caveats: the fierce Mistral winds which rush down the Rhône valley are dry and cold and cause great discomfort, often in March but mainly in the winter. The mosquitoes in the Camargue are a nuisance, and it is suggested you spend the night outside the area, in Arles or Aigues-Mortes. The other problems are man-made. In midsummer crowds of visitors come from all over the world to attend the festivals, and hotels and camp sites are inevitably full, so either make reservations well in advance or plan your visit for early summer or the autumn. Dumas called Marseille 'the meeting place of the entire world' and at night certain areas should not be visited by tourists, who may also find the gypsies of the Camargue a trifle importunate!
Although the French authorities grouped together five large departments to make up modern Provence it is more practical to concentrate on the area of 'Historical Provence' made popular by writers such as

Henry James, Dickens, Wordsworth, Mark Twain, Elizabeth Barrett Browning and Lawrence Durrell. It covers the departments of Bouches-du-Rhône (Marseille, Aix-en-Provence and Arles), the Vaucluse (Orange and Carpentras) and part of Gard (Nîmes, Pont du Gard and Aigues-Mortes). The mighty River Rhône, so strong at Avignon and Arles, meanders into the Mediterranean on both sides of the Camargue, and the lesser-known River Durance starts in the French Alps and runs east to west to join the Rhône south of Avignon. The smaller tributaries of the Sorgue, Nesque and Coulon have good canoeing, and the Rhône itself can be explored by boat cruises from Avignon (near the famous 'Pont d'Avignon') and Arles.

The Greeks occupied the region 2500 years ago, founded Massalia (modern Marseille) and left the olive orchards as a legacy. They were traders, their ships visiting Britain to barter oil and wine for tin, and you can still see a Greek theatre, wall and garden preserved in Marseille.

For five centuries the Romans occupied what they called Provincia and defended it against Hannibal (and his 37 elephants) and armies of Celts and Teutons, until, in 10 BC, Emperor Augustus imposed direct rule. The amphitheatres at Nîmes and Arles date from AD 50, and the Roman theatre at Vaison-la-Romaine dates from AD 1, as does the Capitol (a temple known as La Maison Carrée) in Nîmes. The Pax Romana was most beneficial to the region (certainly to viniculture – Pliny commended the wines of Gigondas) until the decline of the Roman Empire.

Biblical legends abound in Provence, many connected with the Holy Family: Les Saintes-Maries-de-la-Mer is associated with the Virgin Mother's sister, Ste Marie Jacobe, and the mothers of the Apostles James and John, Ste Marie Salomé and Ste Marie Magdaleine; Marseille with Lazare, St. Maximin and St. Victoire; Tarascon with Ste Marthe; and Aix with blind Suedonius.

There is little doubt that in the 3rd-4thC Provence was a notable centre of Christianity. Emperor Constantine held the first council of Christian bishops at Arles in AD 314, and St. Augustin, the first archbishop of Canterbury, was consecrated in the same town in AD 597 by St. Virgil, then Bishop of Arles. Other legends are linked with Apt (St. Anne's shroud), with Les Baux-de-Provence (the Magi or Wise Men of the Nativity) and with Avignon (St. Bénézet, the shepherd bridge-builder).

Provence is most certainly a land of legends and mystery.
During the five centuries after the Romans left, various invaders took it in turn to sack Provence – Visigoths, Vandals, Alemans, Franks, the Saxons in AD 574, the Saracens in AD 726, the Moors, the Normans in the 9thC, and even the Hungarians in AD 924. It is incredible that anybody or anything survived during those dark ages. Fortunately the

Crusaders (mainly French and English) found the southern ports, including Aigues-Mortes, ideal as bases for their armies and fleets bound for the Holy Land, and subsequently the Knights Templars helped restore peace and prosperity and many examples of their 'commanderies' and priories can still be seen. The Counts of Provence and the warrior Lords of Les Baux followed, prosperity returned, and court troubadours sang the praises of their masters and their ladies. When the Papacy transferred from Rome to Avignon early in the 14thC it encouraged not only the arts – musicians, painters and jewellers – but also

architects, who built palaces for 82 cardinals! The incoming Pope, Clement V, became the first serious patron of the arts.

After the papacy returned to Rome, Provence was fortunate to be ruled by the extraordinary 'Good' King René of Anjou (1409-80) who made Aix-en-Provence his capital. A warrior-poet, a bon viveur, musician-painter and grand patron of the arts (he sponsored painters such as Charonton, Froment and Jean Chapuis), he was immensely popular.

But there were dark times too, which perhaps say something about the Provençal character. The Albigensian movement (associated with the Cathars) of the 12th-13thC gained much local support, but the French king ordered Simon de Montfort to exterminate the unfortunate sect. The Protestant Vaudois were massacred in 1545 by the army of King Francis I, and the Huguenots were imprisoned or slaughtered at the Massacre of St. Bartholomew in 1572. Religious wars continued intermittently until the end of the 17thC and towns such as Orange and Nîmes lost half their population. Briefly in 1688 the principality of Orange, part of the Dutch House of Orange Nassau, came under British

sovereignty when William and Mary accepted the British throne. Aix-en-Provence became the home of the exiled Scottish Jacobite court, much visited by the English gentry on its Grand Tour. Indeed, all the Roman antiquities in Arles, Orange and Avignon were normally visited en route for Rome and Naples.

The French Revolution brought only disaster to the region. Castles and churches were pulled down, the clergy, lawyers, mayors and most prominent citizens were executed and the guillotine worked overtime in Marseille. In 1792 500 volunteers from that town marched to Paris singing the song which is now the French national anthem. The French flag – the tricolour – also originated in Provence (blue for Ferrières, red for Jonquières and white for L'Isle), yet Bonaparte received little support from the region and on his way to Elba an attempt was made on his life which caused him to declare, 'C'est une méchante race que les Provençaux' ('These Provençaux are a wicked lot!').

The 19thC brought prosperity to the area with the advent of the railways. Coincidentally, there was an upsurge of interest in local folklore with the creation of the Félibrige, a literary group founded by Frédéric Mistral. He subsequently won a Nobel Prize for literature and dedicated the Muséon Arlaten in Arles, essential for anyone interested in Provençal traditions.

The late 19thC was dominated by the Impressionist painters Paul Cézanne (1839-1906) and Vincent Van Gogh (1853-90) who found inspiration in the ochre-coloured villages, the bleak grandeur of the Ste Victoire mountain range, the cypress trees, golden cornfields and olive groves. Their masterpieces now cost millions and are scattered around the great museums of the world, but they are a living testimony to the dramatic landscape of Provence.

Immaculatæ Virgini Sanctoque Josepho Oblationibus. Benefactorum Nostrorum
Quorum semper in Domino memores erimus

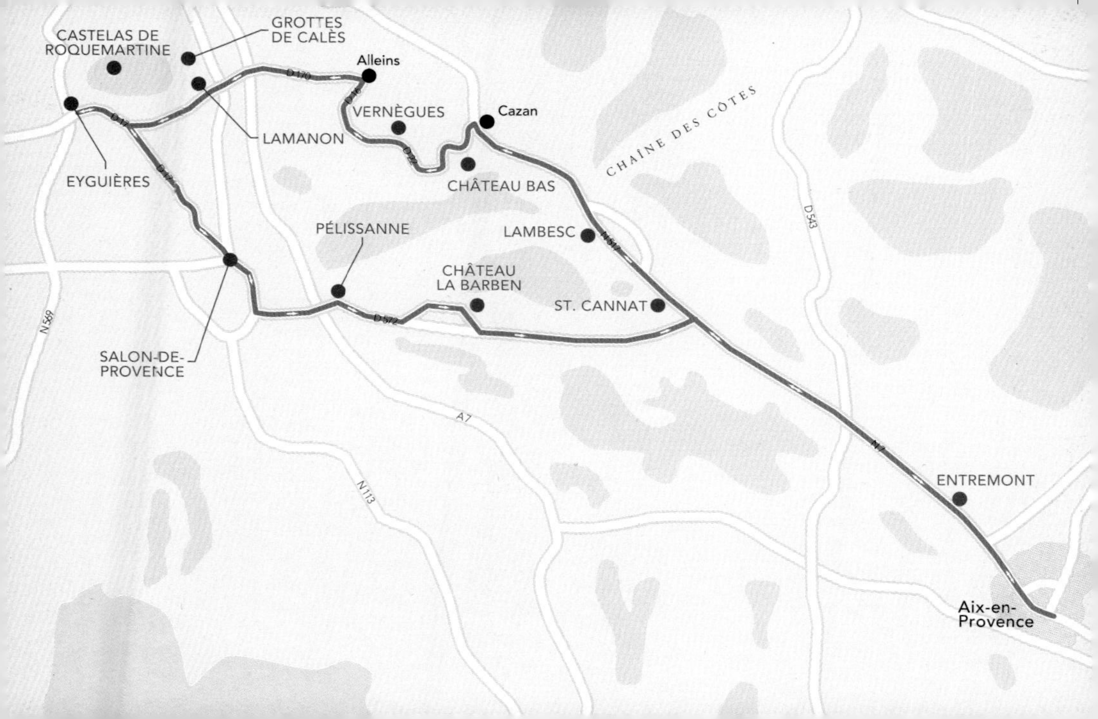
CASTELAS DE ROQUEMARTINE
GROTTES DE CALÈS
Alleins
D170
D16
VERNÈGUES
Cazan
LAMANON
EYGUIÈRES
D17
D22
CHÂTEAU BAS
CHAÎNE DES CÔTES
D543
PÉLISSANNE
LAMBESC
N517
CHÂTEAU LA BARBEN
ST. CANNAT
D572
N569
SALON-DE-PROVENCE
A7
N113
N7
ENTREMONT
Aix-en-Provence

Excursion 1

A half-day excursion northwest to Salon-de-Provence.

Take the N 7 out of Aix, leaving the town and plateau of Entremont (see **A-Z**) on your right, for 16 km to St. Cannat, notable as the home town of the French Admiral Suffren, who frequently defeated the British Royal Navy in the 18thC. Keep to the N 7 but take a detour to Lambesc on the N 517.
21 km – Lambesc (pop: 5000). An old town of considerable charm, with a large church of 14th-18thC provenance. Lambesc was a Resistance HQ in World War II and there was savage fighting in the Chaîne des Côtes, the range of hills to the east. The Château de Montplaisir is a good, moderately-priced hotel/restaurant. Rejoin the N 7 for eight km and turn left in the hamlet of Cazan to the Château Bas and the remains of a Roman temple in a park. Follow the D 22 to Vernègues, a hilltop village ruined by an earthquake in 1909. From the hill overlooking the village you have nearly 360-degree panoramic views of southwest Provence. Drive via the D 16 to Alleins, go west on the D 17 across a canal, and immediately turn left onto the D 17D under the A 7 *autoroute* and the N 538.
43 km – Lamanon. The Calès caves are about 1 km to the north. They were used as an underground fortress by the Celto-Ligurians 2000 years ago. Good views can be had from the top of the hill and it is an excellent place for a picnic. Keep west on the D 17D to Eyguières (pop: 4000) with its many fountains. The ruined Castelas de Roquemartine lies 2 km north on the D 569. Turn southeast for 9 km on the D 17.
52 km – Salon-de-Provence (pop: 36,000). A large rambling market town bisected by the River Craponne and the railway. It is the gateway to La Crau and the melancholy marshland of the upper Camargue to the west. Home of Nostradamus (see **A-Z**) and the engineer De Craponne, who constructed local irrigation channels, Salon has two medieval churches (St. Michel and St. Laurent), the formidable Château de l'Empéri (see **CHATEAUX**) on top of the Puech rocks, and three museums. The Musée de Nostradamus in rue Nostradamus is the 16thC house where the author-astrologer lived and worked (1000-1200, 1500-1900 Wed.-Mon.; 6F). The Musée de Salon et de la Crau is in Ave de Pisavi (1000-1200, 1400-1800 Mon. & Wed.-Fri.; 6F) and the Musée

de l'Empéri in the Château de l'Empéri hous thousands of French military uniforms, flags, medals, etc. from the period 1700-1918 (1000-1200, 1400-1800 Wed.-Mon.; 9F). There are also some excellent restaurants in the town: Fr. Robin, 1 Bd G. Clemenceau, is expensive but Craponne at 146 allées Craponne will serve a moderately-priced meal. The Tourist Information office is situated at 56 cours Gimon, tel: 90562760.

Head east on the D 572 through olive groves to Pélissanne and the 14th-17thC Château la Barben (1000-1200, 1400-1600 Wed.-Mon.; 20F). Napoleon's sister, Pauline Borghese, lived here in splendour amid paintings by Van Loo, Aubusson tapestries and gardens by Le Notre. Children will enjoy the zoo, aviary and aquarium in the 30 ha grounds (1000-1200, 1330-1830; 40F, child 20F). Keep going on the D 572 to St. Cannat and return on the N 7 to Aix-en-Provence.

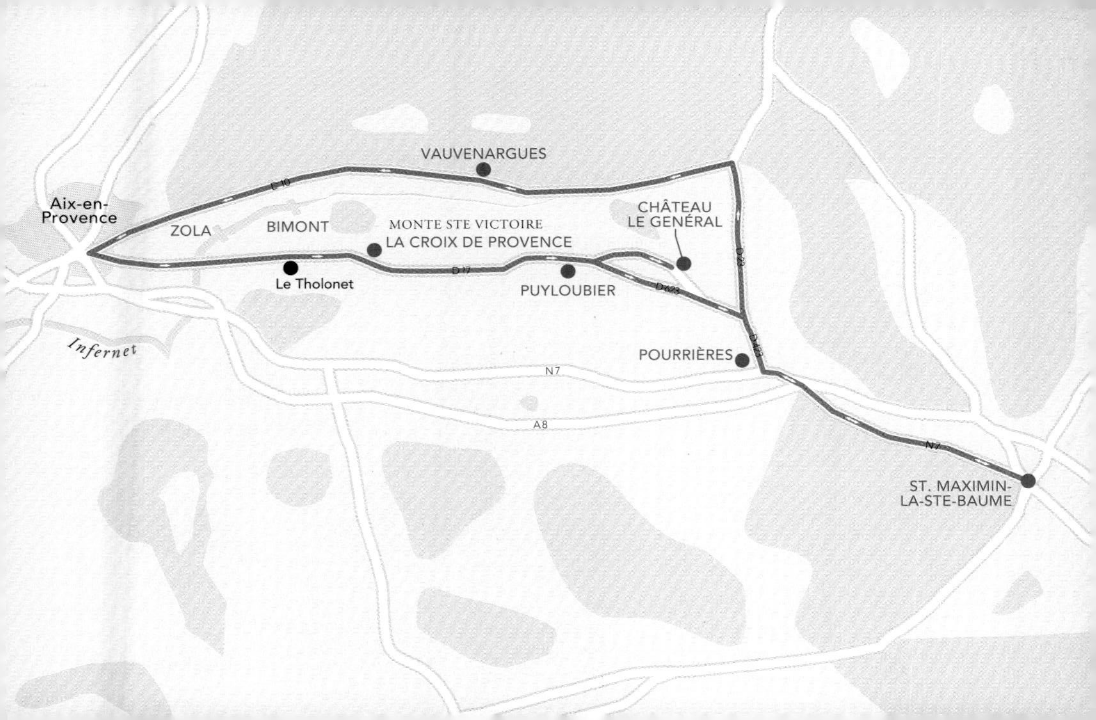
Aix-en-Provence
ZOLA
BIMONT
Le Tholonet
MONTE STE VICTOIRE
LA CROIX DE PROVENCE
VAUVENARGUES
D 10
D 17
PUYLOUBIER
CHÂTEAU LE GENÉRAL
D23
D623
D423
POURRIÈRES
N7
A8
ST. MAXIMIN-LA-STE-BAUME
Infernet

Excursion 2

A half-day excursion east through the landscape painted by Cézanne, to St. Maximin-la-Ste-Baume.

Take the D 17 east to Le Tholonet, past vistas which obsessed Cézanne and are now worth millions on canvas – the Cabanon de Bibemus (quarries), the pine trees around Châteaunoir and many aspects of Monte Ste Victoire. Past the chateau of Le Tholonet on the left is a track which the active can climb to La Croix de Provence (945 m). It takes 1 hr 30 min each way, but don't attempt it in the midday sun.
24 km – Puyloubier. 2.5 km east of the village off the D 57D is the Château Le Genéral, and the Domaine Capitaine Danjou, which is the home of the pensioners of the French Foreign Legion (0900-1200, 1400-1700; 12F). The legion's base is in Aubagne, 40 km south (see **MARSEILLE-EXCURSION 3**). The D 623 leads to Pourrières, a small village with an old fountain, St. Peter's Mill and a Roman tomb called La Trophée de Marius. Follow the D 423 over the A 8 to the N 7 which for 2000 years has been the main road linking Italy, southern France and Spain. The road passes olive groves, pine woods, cork trees and some vineyards dotted with pretty Provençal *mas* or farmhouses.
45 km – The Abbaye de St. Maximin-la-Ste-Baume dominates the small town of the same name. The most important Gothic memorial in Provence, it is closely linked to the legends of Marie Magdaleine and St. Maximin (see **Legends & Myths**). Tradition has it that the former spent the last 33 years of her life sheltering in a cave (*baumo* is 'cave' in Provençal) in a nearby forest. The beautiful but improbable story tells how angels bore her to the summit of the Col du St. Pilon seven times a day to listen to the music of paradise. She and St. Maximin were buried in the crypt under the original church. The present basilica was completed in the 13thC and several kings of France came on pilgrimage. See also the cloisters, chapterhouse and pilgrim hostelry (abbey: open all week; free: cloisters: 1000-1200, 1400-1800; 12F). Head back west towards Aix-en-Provence on the N 7 and D 423. At Pourrières go north on the D 23 and west on the D 10 to the chateau at Vauvenargues (closed to the public) where Picasso (see **A-Z**) is buried in the park. Keep going on the D 10 just north of the River Infernet, past the Bimont and Zola dams, back into Aix-en-Provence.

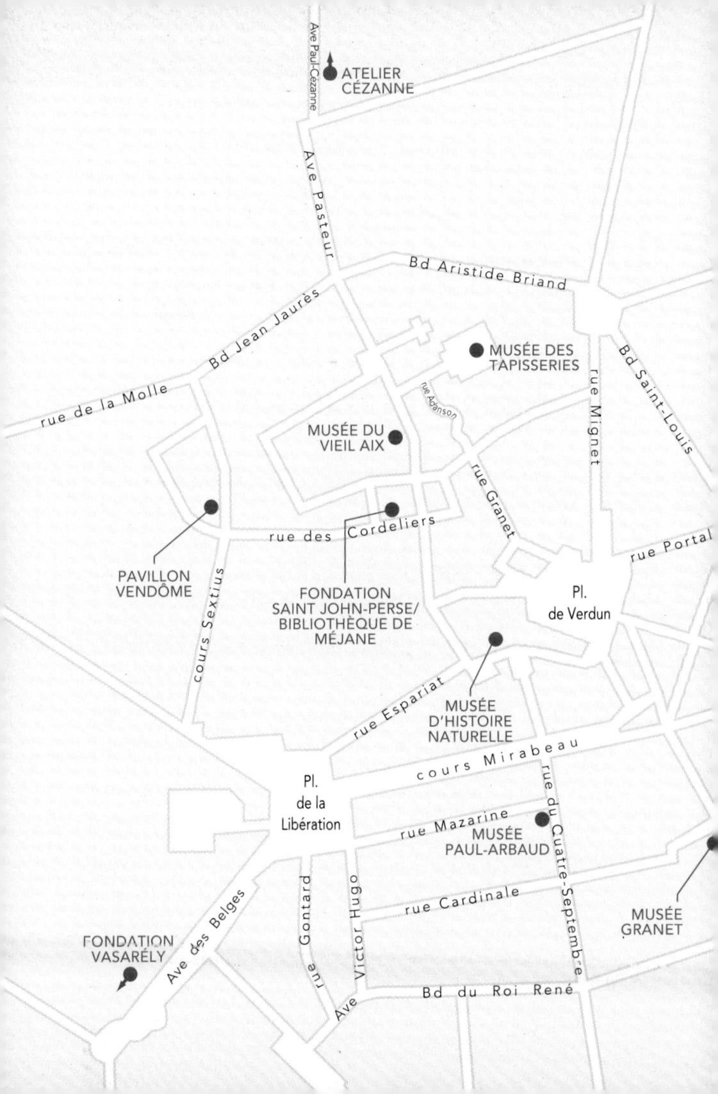
Ave Paul-Cézanne
ATELIER CÉZANNE
Ave Pasteur
Bd Aristide Briand
Bd Jean Jaurès
rue de la Molle
MUSÉE DES TAPISSERIES
rue Adanson
rue Mignet
Bd Saint-Louis
MUSÉE DU VIEIL AIX
rue Granet
rue des Cordeliers
PAVILLON VENDÔME
FONDATION SAINT JOHN-PERSE/ BIBLIOTHÈQUE DE MÉJANE
rue Portal
Pl. de Verdun
cours Sextius
rue Espariat
MUSÉE D'HISTOIRE NATURELLE
cours Mirabeau
Pl. de la Libération
rue Mazarine
MUSÉE PAUL-ARBAUD
rue du Quatre-Septembre
rue Cardinale
MUSÉE GRANET
rue Gontard
Ave Victor Hugo
Ave des Belges
FONDATION VASARÉLY
Bd du Roi René

MUSÉE GRANET (Beaux Arts) Pl. St.-Jean-de-Malte, Quartier Mazarin. Southeast of cours Mirabeau.
❏ 1000-1200, 1400-1800 Wed.-Mon. ❏ 15F.
Housed in the 17thC priory, the Palais de Malte. There is a Cézanne gallery with eight oil paintings, and a rich collection of works by Rembrandt, Rubens and Ingres. One of the finest museums in Provence, it has 500 works contributed by local painter Francois Granet (1775-1849). There is also a collection of Celto-Ligurian archaeological finds from the site at Entremont (see **A-Z**)*, a 2200-year-old fortified village with ramparts, towers, villas and gateways.*

MUSÉE DU VIEIL AIX 17 rue Gaston-de-Saporta, in 17thC Hôtel d'Estienne de St. Jean. 100 m south of the Cathedral.
❏ 1000-1200, 1430-1800 Tue.-Sun. ❏ 13F.
Fine mixed collection from Aix's aristocratic past, arts and traditions, with marionettes, cribs and santons *(see* **A-Z**)*. See King René's pageant-puppet show.*

MUSÉE DES TAPISSERIES ancien Archevêché, Pl. des Martyrs de la Résistance. Near the Cathedral.
❏ 0930-1200, 1430-1830 Wed.-Mon. Closed Jan. ❏ 12F.
17th-18thC Aubusson and Beauvais tapestries by Bérain and Natoire, as well as paintings and antique furnishings.

MUSÉE PAUL-ARBAUD 2a rue du Quatre-Septembre. 100 m south of cours Mirabeau.
❏ 1400-1700 Mon.-Sat. Closed Oct. ❏ 12F.
Collection of faïence, art primitif, *pictures and sculpture. Includes works by Fragonard, Pierre Puget and Granet.*

PAVILLON VENDÔME 32 rue Célony. 100 m west of the Thermal Spa.
❏ 1000-1200, 1430-1830 Wed.-Mon. ❏ 12F.
This is a small collection of 17th-18thC furniture and paintings housed in the beautiful 1667 hôtel *of Cardinal de Vendôme which is situated in a large garden.*

MUSÉE D'HISTOIRE NATURELLE 6 rue Espariat. 100 m north of cours Mirabeau.
❑ 1000-1200, 1400-1800 Mon.-Fri. ❑ 12F.
In 18thC hôtel *Boyer d'Eguilles. Look out for the collection of dinosaur eggs.*

ATELIER CÉZANNE 9 Ave Paul-Cézanne. 1 km north of the Cathedral.
❑ 1000-1200, 1430-1830 Wed.-Mon. ❑ 11F.
The famous Impressionist painter's studio exactly as it was on his death in 1906. *See* AIX-EN-PROVENCE-EXCURSION 2, **Cézanne**.

FONDATION SAINT JOHN-PERSE/BIBLIOTHÈQUE DE MÉJANE Hôtel de Ville, Vieil Aix.
❑ 0900-1200, 1400-1700 Mon.-Fri. ❑ 8F.
Two exhibitions: the first is of the Nobel prize-winning poet's life and work, the second a collection of Provençal literature of the Middle Ages.

FONDATION VASARÉLY Ave Marcel-Pagnol, Jas-de-Bouffan, 4 km west off the D 64.
❑ 0930-1230, 1400-1730 Wed.-Mon. ❑ 25F.
Set in restful gardens, the provocative building houses Hungarian op-art – huge black and white architectural design drawings. An acquired taste, but interesting nonetheless.

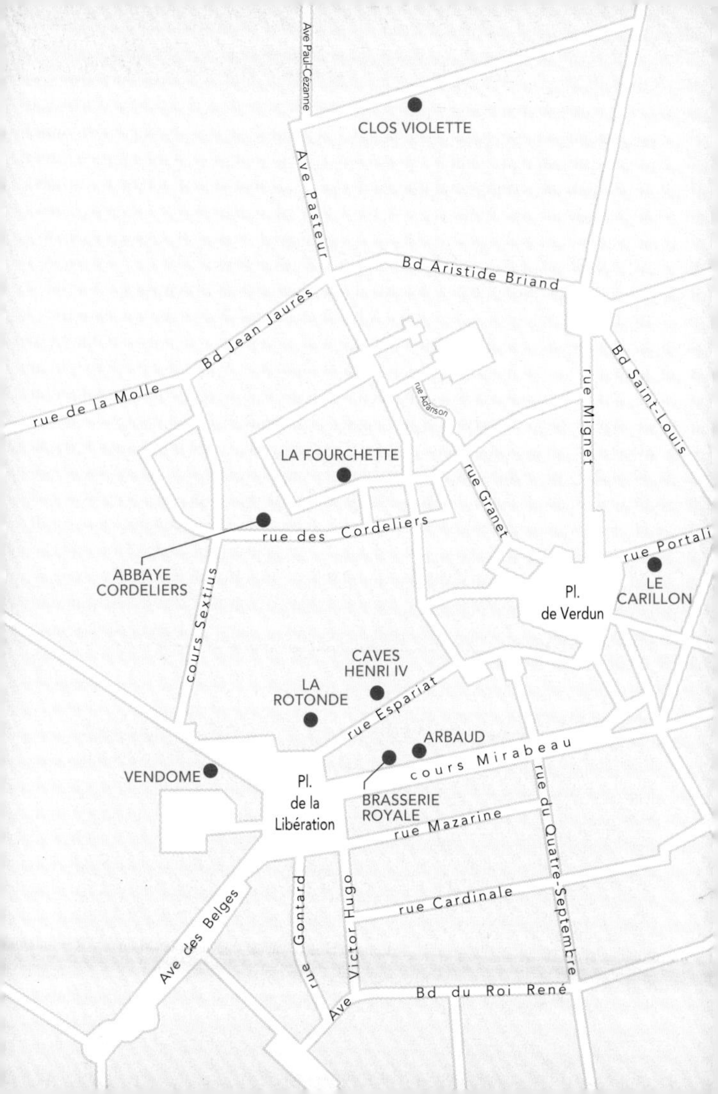
Ave Paul-Cézanne
CLOS VIOLETTE
Ave Pasteur
Bd Aristide Briand
Bd Jean Jaurès
rue de la Molle
rue Adanson
rue Mignet
Bd Saint-Louis
LA FOURCHETTE
rue Granet
rue des Cordeliers
ABBAYE
CORDELIERS
cours Sextius
rue Portalis
LE
CARILLON
Pl.
de Verdun
CAVES
HENRI IV
LA
ROTONDE
rue Espariat
ARBAUD
VENDOME
Pl.
de la
Libération
cours Mirabeau
BRASSERIE
ROYALE
rue Mazarine
rue du Quatre-Septembre
Ave des Belges
rue Gontard
Victor Hugo
rue Cardinale
Ave
Bd du Roi René

VENDÔME 2 bis Ave Napoleon Bonaparte, near the Casino.
❏ 1230-1445, 1930-2230 Thu.-Sun., 1230-1445 Mon. ❏ Expensive.
Classic cuisine. Watch the world go by from the terrace.

CAVES HENRI IV 32 rue Espariat, north of cours Mirabeau.
❏ 1230-1430, 1900-2200 Tue.-Sat. Closed mid June-early July.
❏ Expensive.
Classic cooking and cuisine Provençale, *as well as good wines.*

CLOS VIOLETTE 10 Ave Violette, off Ave Pasteur.
❏ 1200-1430 Tue.-Sat. Closed Aug. ❏ Expensive.
Regional and nouvelle cuisine *in smart surroundings.*

ABBAYE CORDELIERS 21 rue Lieutard, east of cours Sextius.
❏ 1200-1430, 1900-2130 Wed.-Mon. (Mar.-mid Sep.). ❏ Expensive.
Popular restaurant in a 14thC cloister serving nouvelle cuisine.

ARBAUD 19 cours Mirabeau.
❏ 1000-1430, 1900-2400 Tue.-Sun. ❏ Moderate.
Elegant first-floor town hôtel *with elaborate cuisine.*

LA ROTONDE Pl. Jeanne-d'Arc, Vieil Aix.
❏ 1200-1430, 1900-2200 Tue.-Sun. ❏ Moderate.
Restaurant in villa with terrace; serves good Provençal dishes.

BRASSERIE ROYALE 17 cours Mirabeau.
❏ 1145-1445, 1900-2230 Tue.-Sun. ❏ Moderate.
Crowded and informal, on pavement or inside: regional cuisine.

LE CARILLON 10 rue Portalis, Vieil Aix.
❏ 1200-1400, 1900-2230 Tue.-Sun. ❏ Inexpensive.
Good-value prix fixe selection, but very crowded.

LA FOURCHETTE 40 Forum des Cardeurs, Vieil Aix.
❏ 1200-1400, 1930-2400 Mon.-Fri.; Sat.-Sun. pm only. ❏ Inexpensive.
Cheap lunch prix fixe meals served indoors or outdoors.

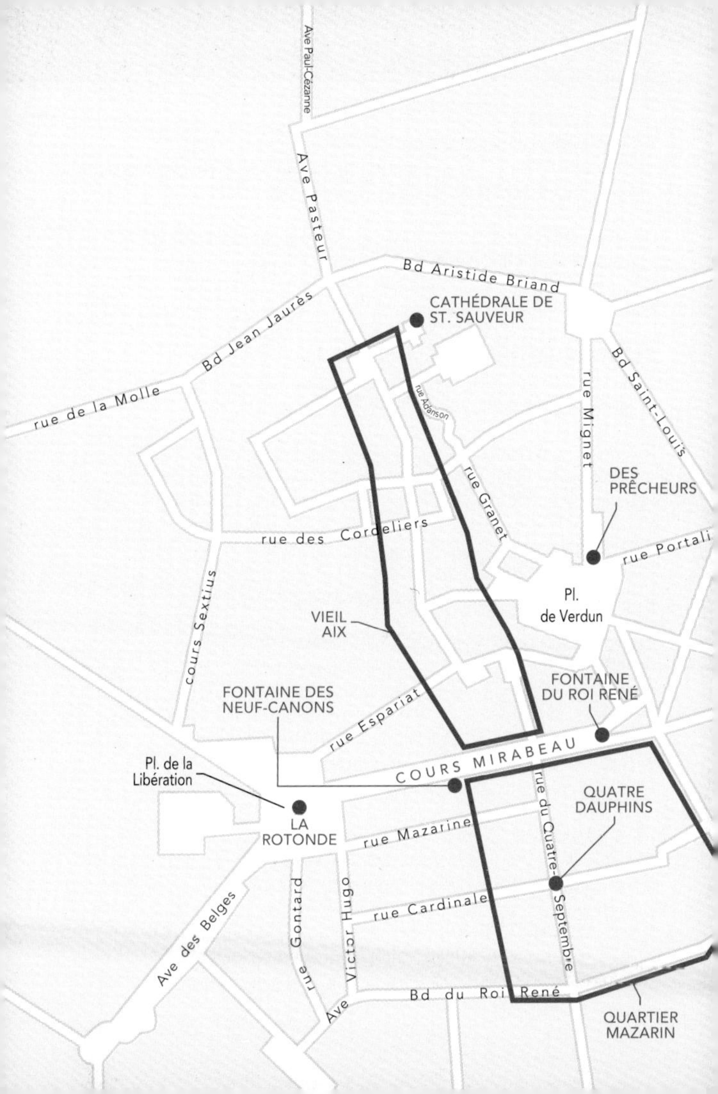
Ave Paul-Cézanne
Ave Pasteur
Bd Aristide Briand
CATHÉDRALE DE
ST. SAUVEUR
Bd Jean Jaurès
rue de la Molle
rue Adanson
rue Mignet
Bd Saint-Louis
rue Granet
DES
PRÊCHEURS
rue des Cordeliers
rue Portali
Pl.
de Verdun
cours Sextius
VIEIL
AIX
FONTAINE
DU ROI RENÉ
FONTAINE DES
NEUF-CANONS
rue Espariat
COURS MIRABEAU
Pl. de la
Libération
LA
ROTONDE
QUATRE
DAUPHINS
rue du Quatre-Septembre
rue Mazarine
rue Cardinale
rue Gontard
Ave Victor Hugo
Ave des Belges
Bd du Roi René
QUARTIER
MAZARIN

COURS MIRABEAU
A famous street, 300 m long, with four rows of plane trees, fountains at each end and in the middle, and lined with elegant 17th-18thC hôtels, *smart shops and cafés.*

VIEIL AIX North of cours Mirabeau to Pl. St. Honoré.
The old town contains the 17thC Hôtel de Ville, 18thC Grain Hall and Archbishop's Palace, 16thC clock tower and several museums.

QUARTIER MAZARIN South of the cours Mirabeau.
*Created by the brother of Cardinal Mazarin. See the National School of Music, the Paul-Arbaud and Granet museums (**see* AIX-EN-PROVENCE-MUSEUMS 1*), and the 13thC priory of the Knights of Malta.*

HÔTELS
There are nearly 160 17th-18thC hôtels *(town mansions) scattered around Aix. Ask for a list from the Tourist Office. Some of the most interesting are in the cours Mirabeau: No. 4, Hôtel de Villars; No. 10, Hôtel d'Entrecasteaux; No. 14, Hôtel de Rousset Boulbon; No. 19, Hôtel d'Arbaud-Jouques; and No. 20, Hôtel de Forbin. One of the oldest is Hôtel Maurel de Pontèves (1650) at 38 rue du Quatre-Septembre.*

CATHÉDRALE DE ST. SAUVEUR rue Gaston de Saporta.
❑ 0800-1200, 1400-1800 Mon.-Sat.; 0900-1900 Sun. ❑ Free.
Architectural styles ranging from 11thC Romanesque to Gothic. The baptistry is 5thC, the belfry 14th-15thC, the beautiful cloister 7th-8thC, and one wall is said to be early Roman! Panels in the west door form a Froment 1476 triptych (tip the verger to see them).

FOUNTAINS
Aix is noted for its 18th-19thC fountains. The largest, La Rotonde, is at the west end of the cours Mirabeau. The 1734 Eau Chaude, 1691 Fontaine des Neuf-Canons and 17thC Fontaine du Roi René form part of the majestic centre and east end of the cours Mirabeau. The 1667 Quatre Dauphins is in the Quartier Mazarin, and the 18thC Des Prêcheurs is near the Église de Ste Marie Magdaleine.

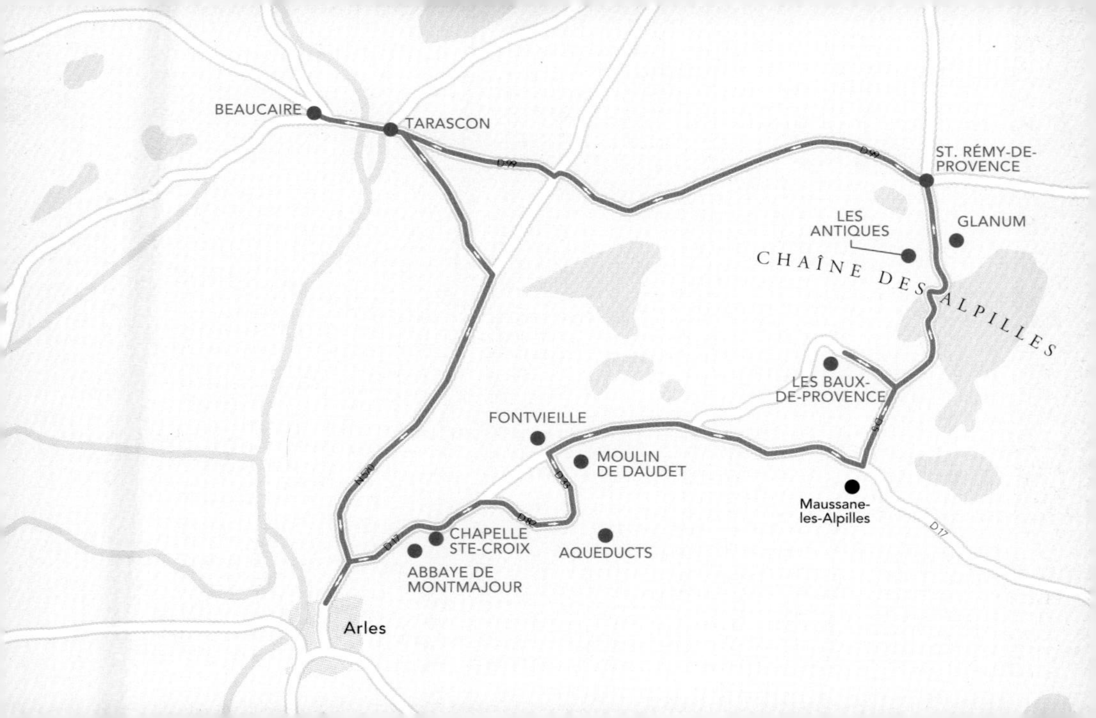
BEAUCAIRE
TARASCON
D99
ST. RÉMY-DE-PROVENCE
LES ANTIQUES
GLANUM
CHAÎNE DES ALPILLES
LES BAUX-DE-PROVENCE
D5
Maussane-les-Alpilles
D17
FONTVIEILLE
MOULIN DE DAUDET
D33
D82
N570
CHAPELLE STE-CROIX
AQUEDUCTS
ABBAYE DE MONTMAJOUR
Arles

A one-day excursion to Les Baux-de-Provence, Roman antiquities, Glanum, St. Rémy-de-Provence and Tarascon.

Leave Arles by the Ave de Stalingrad at the north end of the town and travel 3 km on the N 570, then northeast on the D 17 for another 3 km.
6 km – Abbaye de Montmajour. This is a large, intimidating 10thC Benedictine monastery. The rectangular 12thC towers, Romanesque church, chapel, and cloisters with 360-degree panoramas are well worth a visit. Fortunately Réattu, a local painter, purchased the buildings which the Revolutionaries had wrecked, and restoration is well under way (see **MONASTERIES**). Nearby is the 12thC Chapelle Ste-Croix. Two Gallo-Roman aqueducts which served Arles lie 2 km to the east and are reached by the D 82. 3 km north on the D 33 is the celebrated Moulin de Daudet and small museum (0900-1200, 1400-1900: 7F) (see **Daudet**). Rejoin the D 17.
10 km – Fontvieille (pop: 3500) has eight hotels and several good restaurants, including the expensive La Regalido in rue Frédéric-Mistral and the moderately-priced Le Patio, tel: 90977310. Continue for 10 km east on the D 17 to Maussane-les-Alpilles and north on the D 5 for 2.5 km, then follow a valley road, the D 274, northwest.
28 km – Les Baux-de-Provence (see **A-Z**). A fabulous medieval hilltop village. Leave your car at the foot of the hill outside Porte Mage. The Lords of Les Baux, descended from Balthazar, the Magi king in the 11thC, ruled much of southeast France. They held brilliant troubadour courts of love (see **Troubadours**). Built on a high rocky spur, the citadel was considered impregnable and housed 6000 inhabitants until Louis XIII decided to demolish the Protestant enclave in 1632. The Tourist Office is in the Hôtel de Ville, tel: 90973439 (Easter-Oct.). An entry ticket to the 'Cité Morte', the original town on the crest of the hill, and to the Musée de l'Art Contemporain (Fri.-Wed.) costs 17F. But you can stroll for free around the present village of winding lanes and small squares with elm trees, to see the Église de St. Vincent (12thC); the Chapelle des Pénitents Blancs (17thC); Maison de Manville; Maison de Porcelet; and some superb views. Hotels and restaurants are expensive and the village gets very crowded in the summer season. Take the road over the hills of the Chaîne des Alpilles north towards St. Rémy-de-

D 27A
LES BAUX
45

Provence. After 5 km you will suddenly see, on the left of the road, Les Antiques – two magnificent but isolated Roman statues. The Mausolée has bas-reliefs of Emperor Augustus' grandsons with savage battle scenes and the commemorative arch is vaulted; both date from AD 1. Les Antiques were part of the ceremonial entrance to a large Roman colony a few hundred metres further along on the right, called Glanum. Glanis was the name of the Glanici tribe's god in the 7th-1stC BC. Excavations of mosaics, sculptures, coins and artefacts cover three periods – Celtic, Greek and Roman. The site is 250 m by 100 m and a plan clearly shows the temples, houses, baths, forum and canals (0900-1200, 1400-1800; 25F, half price Sun.). Continue for 1 km north along the D 5.

40 km – St. Rémy-de-Provence (pop: 8500). The St. Paul-de-Mausole monastery and 12thC cloister, where Van Gogh (see **A-Z**) was treated, are at the town entrance on the right of the road. There are two small museums: the Hôtel de Sade and the Pierre de Brun Alpilles. The Tourist Office is in Pl. Jean-Jaurès, tel: 90920522. Continue west on the D 99 for 16 km.

56 km – Tarascon has rivers and marshland to the north and the Chaîne des Alpilles to the south. The Rhône river divides Tarascon from Beaucaire and they have been rival towns for centuries. Beaucaire was a famous trading fair centre in the Middle Ages (see **River Rhône**). The golden castle in Tarascon should be visited (see **CHATEAUX**). The Tarasque folklore street festival with 'monster' and processions takes place on the last Sunday in June (see **Legends & Myths**). Opposite the castle is the small 10thC Église de Ste-Marthe. The saint was the sister of Marie Magdaleine, and reputedly tamed and banished the 'Tarasque'. Despite being bombed in 1944 Tarascon is an attractive little town, approved of by Daudet (see **A-Z**), with several inexpensive restaurants, including St. Jean at 24 Bd Victor-Hugo and Le Provençal, 12 cours Aristide Briand. Visit Beaucaire too if you have the time, with its chateau (see **CHATEAUX**), two interesting museums – Vieux Beaucaire and Lapidaire – and a casino!

It is now 18 km back to Arles via the N 570.

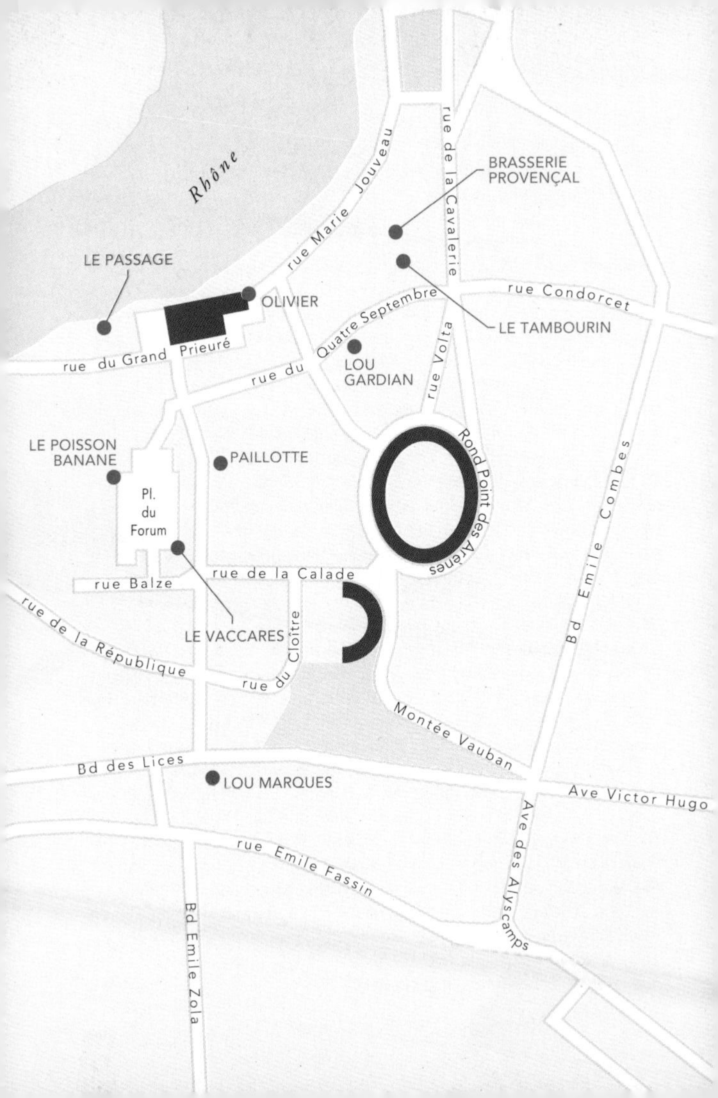
Rhône
rue Marie Jouveau
rue de la Cavalerie
BRASSERIE PROVENÇAL
LE PASSAGE
OLIVIER
rue Condorcet
LE TAMBOURIN
rue du Quatre Septembre
rue du Grand Prieuré
LOU GARDIAN
rue Volta
LE POISSON BANANE
PAILLOTTE
Rond Point des Arènes
Bd Emile Combes
Pl. du Forum
rue de la Calade
rue Balze
rue de la République
LE VACCARES
rue du Cloître
Montée Vauban
Bd des Lices
LOU MARQUES
Ave Victor Hugo
Ave des Alyscamps
rue Emile Fassin
Bd Emile Zola

LOU MARQUES (part of Hotel Jules César) Bd Lices.
❑ 1200-1430, 1900-2100. Closed Nov.-mid Dec. ❑ Expensive.
Excellent regional and nouvelle cuisine.

LE VACCARÈS rue Favorin, off Pl. Forum.
❑ 1200-1400, 1930-2100 Tue.-Sat. Closed late June & mid Dec.-mid Jan. ❑ Moderate.
Provençal cuisine served on a terrace overlooking the square.

PAILLOTTE rue Dr Fanton, near Pl. Forum.
❑ 1200-1400, 1900-2100 Fri.-Tue., 1900-2100 Thu. ❑ Moderate.
Restaurant with an elegant ambience; river fish a speciality.

OLIVIER 1 rue Réattu, near the Museum.
❑ 1200-1430, 1900-2130 Tue.-Sat., 1900-2130 Mon. ❑ Moderate.
Nouvelle cuisine *and good-value prix fixe menus.*

BRASSERIE PROVENÇAL 38 rue Amedée-Pichot.
❑ 1145-1430, 1900-2200 Mon.-Sat. Closed June. ❑ Moderate.
Typical Provençal brasserie: good cheerful fare – grills, steaks and fish.

LE TAMBOURIN 65 rue Amedée-Pichot, north of the Arena.
❑ 1200-1400, 2000-2200 Sun.-Fri. Closed Feb. ❑ Moderate.
Camargue dishes with rice: try boeuf gardien.

LOU GARDIAN 70 rue du Quatre Septembre, north of the Arena.
❑ 1200-1430, 1930-2200 Mon.-Sat. ❑ Inexpensive.
Popular, family-run restaurant serving Provençal cuisine.

LE POISSON BANANE 6 rue du Forum.
❑ 1200-1430, 1645-2230 Mon.-Sat. ❑ Inexpensive.
Eccentric restaurant with a youthful atmosphere and unusual dishes.

LE PASSAGE Quai Max Dormoy, near River Rhône.
❑ 1200-1400, 1900-2200 Tue.-Sun. ❑ Inexpensive.
Café, restaurant, bookstore, cinema and picture gallery all in one!

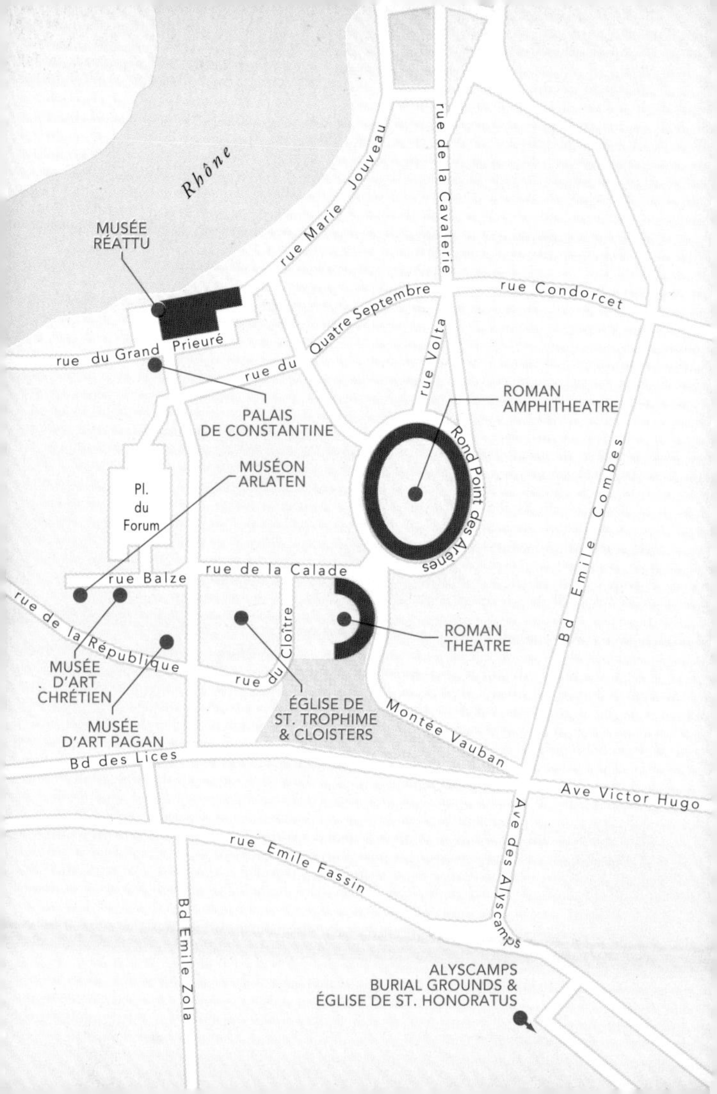
Rhône
MUSÉE RÉATTU
rue Marie Jouveau
rue de la Cavalerie
rue Condorcet
rue du Quatre Septembre
rue du Grand Prieuré
rue Volta
ROMAN AMPHITHEATRE
PALAIS DE CONSTANTINE
Rond Point des Arènes
MUSÉON ARLATEN
Pl. du Forum
Bd Emile Combes
rue Balze
rue de la Calade
rue de la République
rue du Cloître
ROMAN THEATRE
MUSÉE D'ART CHRÉTIEN
MUSÉE D'ART PAGAN
ÉGLISE DE ST. TROPHIME & CLOISTERS
Montée Vauban
Bd des Lices
Ave Victor Hugo
rue Emile Fassin
Ave des Alyscamps
Bd Emile Zola
ALYSCAMPS BURIAL GROUNDS & ÉGLISE DE ST. HONORATUS

ÉGLISE DE ST. TROPHIME & CLOISTERS
rue l'Hôtel de Ville.
❑ 1000-1200, 1600-1900. ❑ Church free; cloisters 17F.
Romanesque 11th-12thC church with a vaulted nave, west doorway, golden square belfry, lovely galleries in the cloisters, tapestries and Christian sarcophagi.

ROMAN AMPHITHEATRE (Arènes)
❑ 0830-1900 May-Sep.; 0900-1200, 1400-1700 Oct.-April. ❑ 12F.
Built in AD 1 for Emperor Augustus and one of the largest surviving arenas in France. It is 107 m by 136 m. Panoramic views. Used for bullfights Easter-autumn. See **Arles**, **Bullfights**.

ROMAN THEATRE rue du Cloître, 100 m southwest of the Roman Amphitheatre.
❑ 0900-1200, 1400-1700. ❑ 9F.
Built circa 1 BC by Emperor Augustus, the theatre could hold 7000 spectators. Much pillaged for stone in the Middle Ages, imagination is now needed to recreate it in its original dramatic site. The stage wall and foundations, 100 m wide, and the 20 remaining rows of stone seats give some clues. See **Arles**.

MUSÉON ARLATEN Corner of rue Frédéric Mistral and rue de la République.
❑ 0900-1200, 1400-1800. Closed Mon. out of season. ❑ 10F.
Provençal folklore museum, founded by 19thC poet Frédéric Mistral (see **A-Z***). Costumes, paintings, living rooms, prints, pottery and furniture of bygone eras exhibited in 16thC* hôtel*; staff dress in authentic old Provençal clothing. See* **Félibrige**.

MUSÉE RÉATTU On river bank, in Grand Prieuré des Chevaliers de St. Jean de Jerusalem.
❑ 0900-1200, 1400-1800. ❑ 15F.
Works include Provençal School painters, Rousseau's views of the Camargue, Picasso (see **A-Z***) drawings and several hundred works by local painter Jacques Réattu. Photographic display on first floor.*

CLUB CLUB CLUB
STELLA ARTOIS
STELLA ARTOIS

PALAIS DE CONSTANTINE rue D. Maisto, near Musée Réattu.
❑ 0900-1200, 1400-1700. ❑ 12F.
A slight misnomer. Really part of the Roman public baths, 98 m by 45 m, built c.4thC as part of Emperor Constantine's huge palace. Clients had a choice of frigidarium, tepidarium or calidarium. See **Arles**.

MUSÉE D'ART PAGAN Plan de la Cour.
❑ 0900-1200, 1400-1800. ❑ 7F.
Pre-Christian mosaics and archaeological finds housed in the 17thC Église de Ste Anne.

MUSÉE D'ART CHRÉTIEN
rue Balze.
❑ 0900-1200, 1400-1800. ❑ 7F.
This museum consists largely of a lapidary collection and a crypt in a 17thC Jesuit chapel.

TOWN RAMPARTS
600 m of wall still exists in the southeast of the town, between the Bd des Lices and Bd Emile Combes, and a further 300 m at the north end of the town (including the Porte de la Cavalrie).

ALYSCAMPS BURIAL GROUNDS & ÉGLISE DE ST. HONORATUS
1.5 km southeast of Tourist Office.
❑ 0900-1200, 1400-1800. ❑ 7F.
Roman necropolis, situated near the canal, much painted by Vincent Van Gogh (see **A-Z***). Some sarcophagi from the site are now housed in the Musée d'Art Chrétien (see above). See* **Arles**.

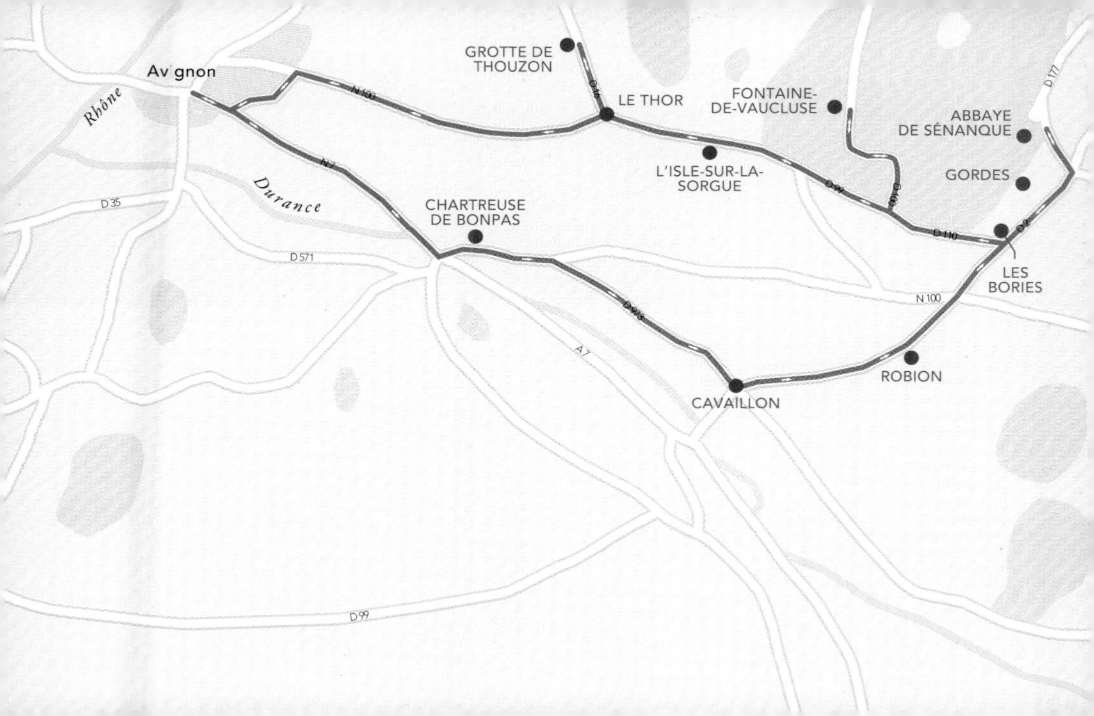
Av gnon
Rhône
Durance
GROTTE DE THOUZON
LE THOR
FONTAINE-DE-VAUCLUSE
ABBAYE DE SÉNANQUE
GORDES
L'ISLE-SUR-LA-SORGUE
CHARTREUSE DE BONPAS
LES BORIES
CAVAILLON
ROBION
N 100
N 7
D 16
D 99
D 100
D 110
D 2
D 177
D 35
D 571
D 973
A 7

A one-day excursion to Chartreuse de Bonpas, Cavaillon, Gordes, the Abbaye de Sénanque, Fontaine-de-Vaucluse, L'Isle-sur-la-Sorgue and Le Thor.

Leave Avignon on the N 7 southeast for 11 km passing the municipal swimming pool (*piscine*) and the airport of Avignon-Caumont. Go under the A 7 and on the left you will see the Chartreuse de Bonpas, a 13thC Templar charterhouse, chapel and porter's lodge (1000-1700; 8F). Continue on the D 973 for 13 km.

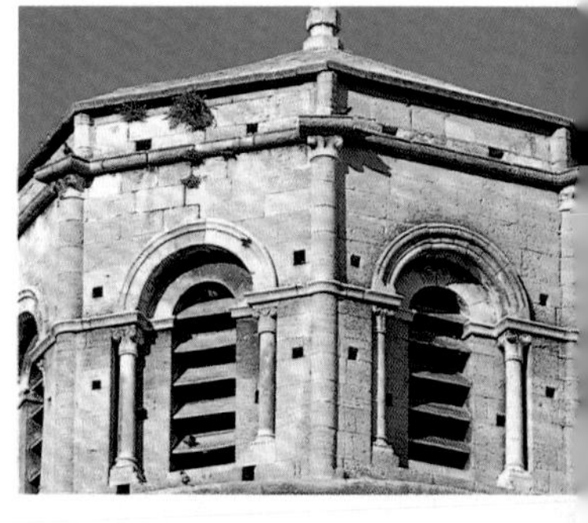

24 km – Cavaillon (pop: 21,000). The sweet, rose-pink melons in the surrounding market gardens have made Cavaillon prosperous (see **River Rhône**). The 18thC Jewish synagogue (see **Synagogues**) and museum is in rue Hébraique (0900-1200, 1400-1800 Wed.-Mon.; 7F). The Musée Municipal in Grand Rue, with its archaeological collection and late medieval hospital mementoes, should also be seen (1000-1200, 1400-1800 Wed.-Mon.; 7F). The Cathédrale de St. Véran houses an historic organ and has 12thC cloisters. The best views can be obtained from St. Jacques Hill, on the west side of town near the Arc Romain. *Cuisine Provençale* is inexpensive at Restaurant Toppin, 70 cours Gambetta.

Take the D 2 towards Apt. At the crossroads with the N 100 (past the village of Robion) keep straight ahead uphill on the D 2 for 9 km.

42 km – Gordes (pop: 1800). The Renaissance chateau now houses the Vasarély art collection (see CHATEAUX). The stone houses, shaded cafés and expensive restaurants on the 400 m spur combine to make Gordes one of the prettiest of Provençal villages. The 12thC Cistercian Abbaye de Sénanque is in a narrow, lavender-filled valley 7 km north on the D 177. Now well restored, the abbey is also a cultural centre

Fontaine-de-Vaucluse

with the institutes for Medieval Studies, and of African Toureg tribes, as well as hosting summer concerts of medieval music (see **MONASTERIES, Petrarch**). Head south past Gordes.

52 km – Les Bories. These stone-built, beehive-shaped huts were probably a medieval refuge for town dwellers fleeing from the plague. A small museum of Provençal rural life is at the end of the lane (2 km) (0900-1630; 13F). Now drive westwards continuing on the D 110 and D 100 for 10 km.

62 km – Fontaine-de-Vaucluse (see **A-Z**): park in the village. It can get very crowded in midsummer as visitors come to see the natural wonder of the Vaucluse department: the source of the Sorgue river, which wells up with amazing velocity from the foot of high cliffs. The ten-minute walk parallel to the new-born river, from the village to the source, is extremely pleasant. There are *Son et Lumière* in midsummer at 2130. There is another, more romantic, reason for a visit. The 14thC Italian poet Petrarch took up residence in the village for 16 years and it was here that he composed his famous *Canzonière* addressed to 'Laura', a married lady from Avignon (see **Petrarch**). Norbert Casteret's Musée de Spéléologie on the chemin de la Fontaine is the potholing museum of the Vaucluse (1000-1230, 1400-1900 summer only; 9F). Restaurant La Rascasse d'Argent, rte de Fontaine-de-Vaucluse, is moderately priced and specializes in fish dishes. Follow the D 99 and N 100 west for 7 km.

69 km – L'Isle-sur-la-Sorgue (pop: 13,000) is nicknamed 'The Venice of Provence' because of its five rivers and canals. The town features a 17thC church with rich Italianate paintings by Mignard and Parrocel, both of Provence, and a 17thC hospital, an 18thC fountain and Renaissance houses, all combining to make L'Isle-sur-la-Sorgue a restful oasis in the hot Provençal summer. The restaurants La Guinguette and Le Pescador serve inexpensive meals featuring local freshwater trout. The July festival includes water-jousting competitions and horse races. Continue for 6 km west on the N 100 to Le Thor (famous for its white Chasselas dessert grapes) then take the D 16 north for 3 km.

78 km – Grotte de Thouzon. Nearly 300 m of caves with stalactites can be seen (0900-1200, 1330-1900 summer, afternoons only in winter; 17F). Return on the N 100 for 18 km to Avignon.

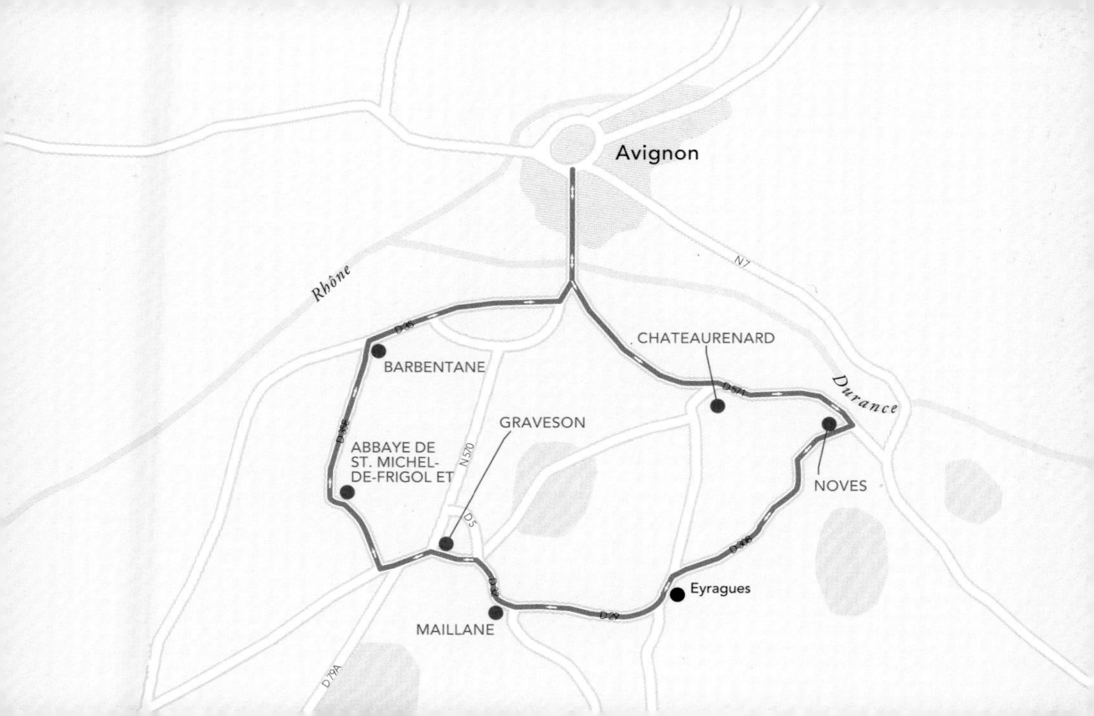
Avignon
Rhône
N7
CHATEAURENARD
Durance
D571
BARBENTANE
GRAVESON
ABBAYE DE
ST. MICHEL-
DE-FRIGOL ET
N570
NOVES
D5
Eyragues
MAILLANE
D79A

Excursion 2

A half-day excursion southwest to Noves, Maillane, the Abbaye de St. Michel-de-Frigolet and Barbentane.

Head due south on the D 571 for 4 km crossing the River Durance and then head southeast.
6 km – Chateaurenard (pop: 11,000). The town rivals Cavaillon with its produce (see **AVIGNON-EXCURSION 1**). The 14thC Griffon tower is one of two, part of a feudal castle, with superb views (1000-1200, 1400-1900; 5F). Four unusual fêtes associated with bull fighting are held here each year. Restaurant Les Glycines at 14 Ave V. Hugo is inexpensive but closed on Mondays. Drive east for 6.5 km on the D 28.
16.5 km – Noves (pop: 4000) has the 12thC large-domed Église de St. Baudile, medieval streets and gateways. The Auberge de Noves is an expensive hotel-restaurant which serves the local wines, Côteaux des Baux and Côteaux du Lubéron. 6thC BC coins and ceramics have been excavated here, also a pre-Roman sculpture of the 'Tarasque de Noves', the fabulous monster – half crocodile, half lion – linked with Ste Marthe of Tarascon (see **ARLES-EXCURSION**, **Legends & Myths**). Go south on the D 30B for 7 km to Eyragues, then 5 km on the D 29 and D 32.
28.5 km – Maillane (pop: 1500) was the home town of Frédéric Mistral, one of Provence's most famous citizens. The Muséon Mistral is one of two museums dedicated to the Nobel prize-winning poet (1000-1200, 1400-1700 Tue.-Sun.; 8F), the other being the Arlaten in Arles (see **ARLES-WHAT TO SEE 1**, **Félibrige**, **Mistral**). Continue northwest for 3 km on the D 5 to Graveson (pop: 2500). A pilgrimage takes place on 27 April to the Église de St. Anthime (see **Pilgrimages**). Drive southwest for 2 km to the minor D 81 and follow it for 3 km.
37 km – Abbaye de St. Michel-de-Frigolet (see **MONASTERIES**). Founded in the 10thC by the Montmajour monks. It is idyllically sited among pine woods, olive groves and cypress, with the Église de St. Michel, 12thC abbey cloisters, chapel, museum, pilgrim hostels and a small restaurant. Go north on the minor D 35E for 6 km.
43 km – Barbentane (pop: 3500) has two medieval gateways, 17thC town houses, and the 17thC chateau of the Dukes of Barbentane with classic facades and rich Louis XV and XVI furnishings (see **CHATEAUX**). Return eastwards on the D 35 for 12.5 km to Avignon.

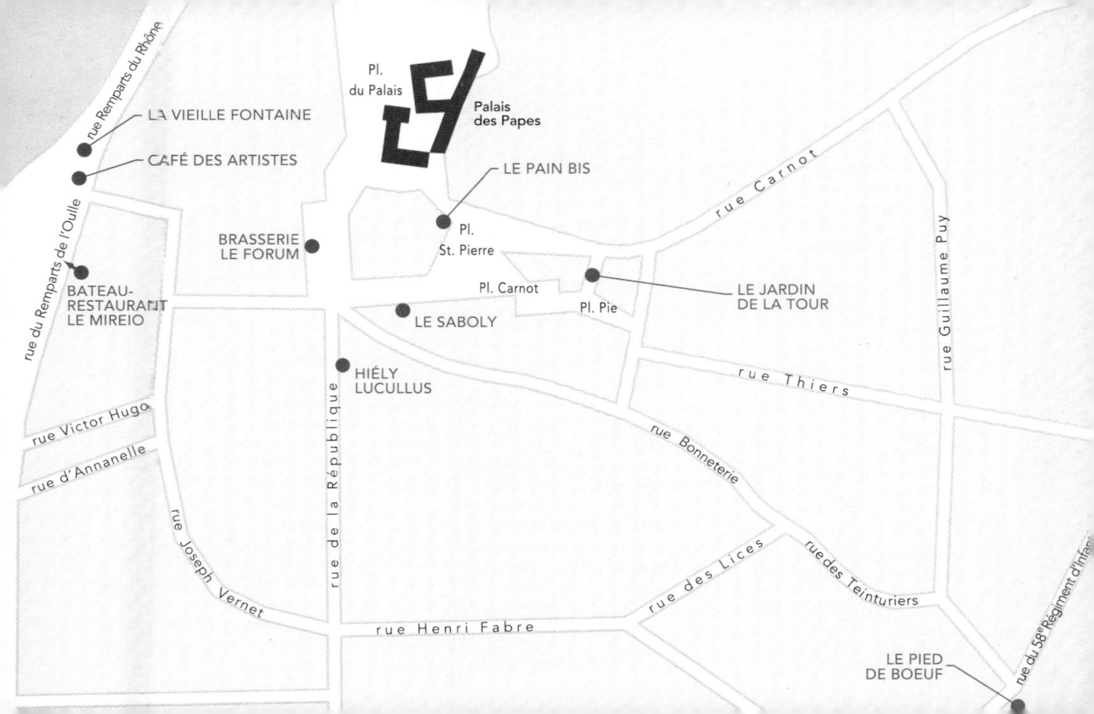
rue Remparts du Rhône
LA VIEILLE FONTAINE
CAFÉ DES ARTISTES
Pl.
du Palais
Palais
des Papes
LE PAIN BIS
rue Carnot
BRASSERIE
LE FORUM
Pl.
St. Pierre
rue du Remparts de l'Oulle
BATEAU-
RESTAURANT
LE MIREIO
Pl. Carnot
LE JARDIN
DE LA TOUR
Pl. Pie
LE SABOLY
rue Guillaume Puy
HIÉLY
LUCULLUS
rue Thiers
rue Victor Hugo
rue Bonneterie
rue d'Annanelle
rue de la République
rue Joseph Vernet
rue des Lices
rue des Teinturiers
rue Henri Fabre
LE PIED
DE BOEUF
rue du 58e Régiment d'Infa

HIÉLY LUCULLUS 5 rue de la République, near Hôtel de Ville.
❑ 1200-1400, 1945-2115. Closed Jan., Mar. & late June. ❑ Expensive.
Haute cuisine*: try* moules aux épinards *and* tourte de cailles.

LA VIEILLE FONTAINE 12 Pl. Crillon, in Hôtel de l'Europe on east side of Pont Ed. Daladier.
❑ 1930-2200. Closed Jan., mid-Aug. & early Nov. ❑ Expensive.
Classic cuisine near an old fountain. Try rizotto de pigeon aux truffes.

LE JARDIN DE LA TOUR 9 rue de la Tour, in town centre.
❑ 1200-1400, 1945-2200. Closed late Aug. ❑ Moderate.
Cuisine Provençale*: try the* cabri du Luberon.

LE PIED DE BOEUF 49 Ave Pierre Sémard.
❑ 1200-1400, 1945-2200 Mon.-Sat. Closed July. ❑ Moderate.
Restaurant serving traditional cuisine, including estouffade de canard.

BRASSERIE LE FORUM (Café-théatre) 20 Pl. de l'Horloge.
❑ 1200-2300. ❑ Moderate.
Traditional fare: try magret de canard poelé au jus de porto.

CAFÉ DES ARTISTES 21 bis Pl. Crillon.
❑ 1200-1400, 1900-2200 Mon.-Sat. Closed early Jan. ❑ Moderate.
Traditional and Provençal cuisine, including lapin à l'ail.

BÂTEAU-RESTAURANT LE MIREIO allées de l'Oulle.
❑ 1200-1400, 1900-2400. Closed mid Jan.-mid Feb. ❑ Moderate.
Fish dishes – try saumon mariné *– served on a Rhône cruiser.*

LE SABOLY (Café-théatre) 4 Pl. Nicolas Saboly near Pl. de l'Horloge.
❑ 1200-1400, 1900-2400 (2030-2400 Wed.-Fri.). ❑ Inexpensive.
Provençal-style moules marinières *and* truite aux amandes.

LE PAIN BIS 6 rue Armand-de-Pontmartin, near Pl. St. Pierre.
❑ 1200-1430, 1900-2400 Mon.-Sat. ❑ Inexpensive.
A restaurant specializing in vegetarian dishes.

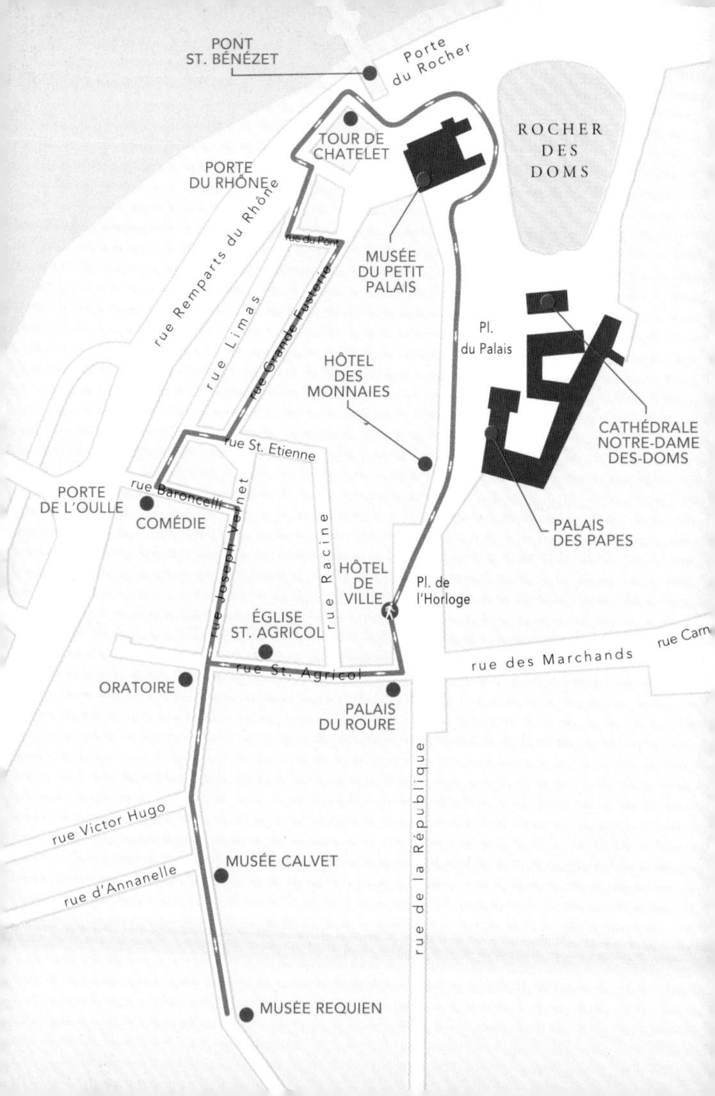
PONT
ST. BÉNÉZET
Porte
du Rocher
TOUR DE
CHATELET
ROCHER
DES
DOMS
PORTE
DU RHÔNE
rue Remparts du Rhône
rue du Pont
MUSÉE
DU PETIT
PALAIS
rue Limas
rue Grande Fusterie
Pl.
du Palais
HÔTEL
DES
MONNAIES
CATHÉDRALE
NOTRE-DAME
DES-DOMS
rue St. Etienne
PORTE
DE L'OULLE
rue Baroncelli
COMÉDIE
rue Joseph Vernet
rue Racine
PALAIS
DES PAPES
HÔTEL
DE
VILLE
Pl. de
l'Horloge
ÉGLISE
ST. AGRICOL
rue Carn
rue des Marchands
rue St. Agricol
ORATOIRE
PALAIS
DU ROURE
rue de la République
rue Victor Hugo
MUSÉE CALVET
rue d'Annanelle
MUSÉE REQUIEN

2 hr-2 hr 30 min (depending on guided visits).

Start at the 19thC Hôtel de Ville, known as Jacquemart, in the Pl. de l'Horloge. Turn right and second right into the rue St. Agricol. The Palais du Roure, a handsome 15thC palace once owned by Baron de Baroncelli, is on the corner (3 rue du Collège-du-Roure). The Baron was instrumental in reviving the Camargue and its customs. At 19 rue St. Agricol is a bookshop, Librairie Roumanille, specializing in Provençal literature. At No. 23 the Hôtel du Louvre has the remains of the 11thC Knights Templars' Commanderie. Their chapel faces the Église St. Agricol, founded by the patron saint of the city in the 7thC and rebuilt under Pope Jean XII in the 14thC. At the end of the road is a crossroads with rue Joseph Vernet – the Musée Calvet (see **AVIGNON-WHAT TO SEE**) and Musée Requien are 250 m on the left. Straight ahead is the Oratoire with its splendid baroque facade, which houses the Chapelles des Pénitents Gris et Noirs, (1730-48).
Keep north up rue Joseph Vernet for 100 m. At Nos 21-23 Bonaparte wrote the *Souper de Beaucaire*, and at Nos 7-11 is the Hôtel de Tonduti de Malijac. Walk left and west via rue Baroncelli to the handsome Pl. Crillon and the Porte de l'Oulle (leading to the Pont Daladier, with superb views, which crosses the Rhône towards Villeneuve-lès-Avignon). The remains of Avignon's first theatre, the Comédie, built in 1732 of Fontvieille stone, are visible. In the Pl. Crillon are two old town *hôtels* – Hôtel du Palais Royal and Hôtel Amat de Graveson (now the Hôtel d'Europe). Head north on rue du Limas and right into rue St. Etienne. La Maison des Forli at Nos 22-24 is 16thC (now a print gallery), and at No. 18, Maison aux Ballons, Joseph de Montgolfier first conceived his hot-air balloon theory. In the rue Grande Fusterie are the Hôtel de Tertulle at Nos 8-10 and the Maison du Pagadour at Nos 63-65. Now go left on rue du Pont, right again on rue Limas and left through the Porte du Rhône gate and ramparts to see the Rhône and the Pont St. Bénézet. The small chapel on the 12thC bridge is dedicated to St. Nicolas, patron saint of mariners. If you want to walk, sing or dance on the bridge a small souvenir shop beneath it will sell you a ticket (see **AVIGNON-WHAT TO SEE**). The Tour de Chatelet, a small 14thC fortress which served as the eastern bridge defence, gives access to the rampart

Jardin du Rocher des Doms

walk leading to the Jardin du Rocher des Doms (see **AVIGNON-WHAT TO SEE**). You may like to spend some time in these pretty, friendly gardens with panoramic views – a photographer's dream.
Descend by the western side steps to the 14thC Musée du Petit Palais to see the Italian (250 primitives in the Campana collection) and Provençal works of art (see **AVIGNON-WHAT TO SEE**). Go south along the Pl. du Palais and on your left is the mighty Palais des Papes, one of the largest medieval fortresses in the world, visited by half a million people each year. Pierre Poisson built the austere Old Palace and Jean de Louvres the New Palace with its magnificent Champeaux Gate. A guided visit takes 1 hr (see **AVIGNON-WHAT TO SEE**, **Palais des Papes**, **Papacy at Avignon**). The 12thC Cathédrale de Notre-Dame-des-Doms is next door. It has a beautiful Romanesque porch, and frescoes by Simone Martini of Sienna. Look out for the tomb of Pope John XXII (see **AVIGNON-WHAT TO SEE**).
On the way back to the Pl. de l'Horloge, where the Jacquemart statues on the top of the clock tower sound the hours, notice the Hôtel des Monnaies built in 1619. This mint once housed Cardinal Borghese and is now Avignon's Conservatoire of Music.

Palais des Papes

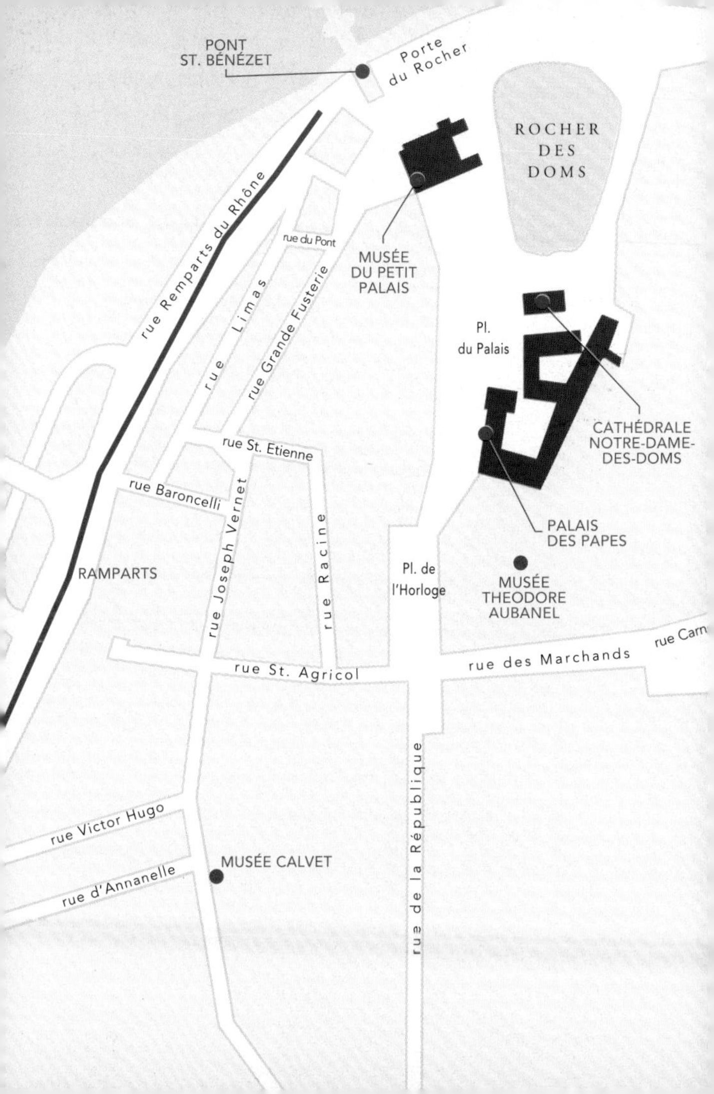
PONT
ST. BÉNÉZET
Porte
du Rocher
ROCHER
DES
DOMS
rue Remparts du Rhône
rue du Pont
MUSÉE
DU PETIT
PALAIS
rue Limas
rue Grande Fusterie
Pl.
du Palais
CATHÉDRALE
NOTRE-DAME-
DES-DOMS
rue St. Etienne
rue Baroncelli
rue Joseph Vernet
rue Racine
PALAIS
DES PAPES
RAMPARTS
Pl. de
l'Horloge
MUSÉE
THEODORE
AUBANEL
rue St. Agricol
rue des Marchands
rue de la République
rue Victor Hugo
rue d'Annanelle
MUSÉE CALVET

PALAIS DES PAPES Pl. du Palais.
❑ 0900-1815 July-Sep.; 0900-1115,1400-1715 Oct.-June.
❑ Guided Tours 30F.
The major architectural sight in Provence. The Popes' palace and fortress during the 14thC. See AVIGNON-WALK, **Palais des Papes**, **Papacy at Avignon**.

PONT ST. BÉNÉZET rue Ferruce.
❑ 0900-1200, 1400-1900. ❑ 8F.
12thC bridge made famous by the song Sur le pont d'Avignon. *Only four of the original 22 arches have survived. The best view of the bridge is from the Rocher des Doms gardens. See* AVIGNON-WALK, **River Rhône**.

CATHÉDRALE DE NOTRE-DAME-DES-DOMS Next to Palais.
❑ 0800-1800.
Provençal Romanesque-style church containing the tomb of Pope John XXII, and a richly decorated interior. See AVIGNON-WALK.

MUSÉE DU PETIT PALAIS Next to Palais.
❑ 0915-1150, 1400-1800 Wed.-Mon. ❑ 16F.
14thC residence of Cardinal of Avignon. 15thC Avignon paintings, 13th-16thC Italianate and Romanesque sculpture. See AVIGNON-WALK.

MUSÉE CALVET 65 rue Joseph Vernet.
❑ 1000-1200, 1400-1800 Wed.-Mon. ❑ 16F.
17th-18thC Flemish and French collection of paintings, antiquities and ironwork (gates, locks, etc.). See AVIGNON-WALK.

MUSÉE THÉODORE AUBANEL Pl. St. Pierre.
❑ 0900-1200 Mon.-Fri. Closed Aug. ❑ 10F.
Provençal literature and printing works. See **Félibrige**.

RAMPARTS
Constructed in the 14thC, 10 km of walls survive with 15 town gates. A walk goes from the Tour de Chatelet to the Jardin du Rocher des Doms, near the River Rhône, on the north side of town. See AVIGNON-WALK.

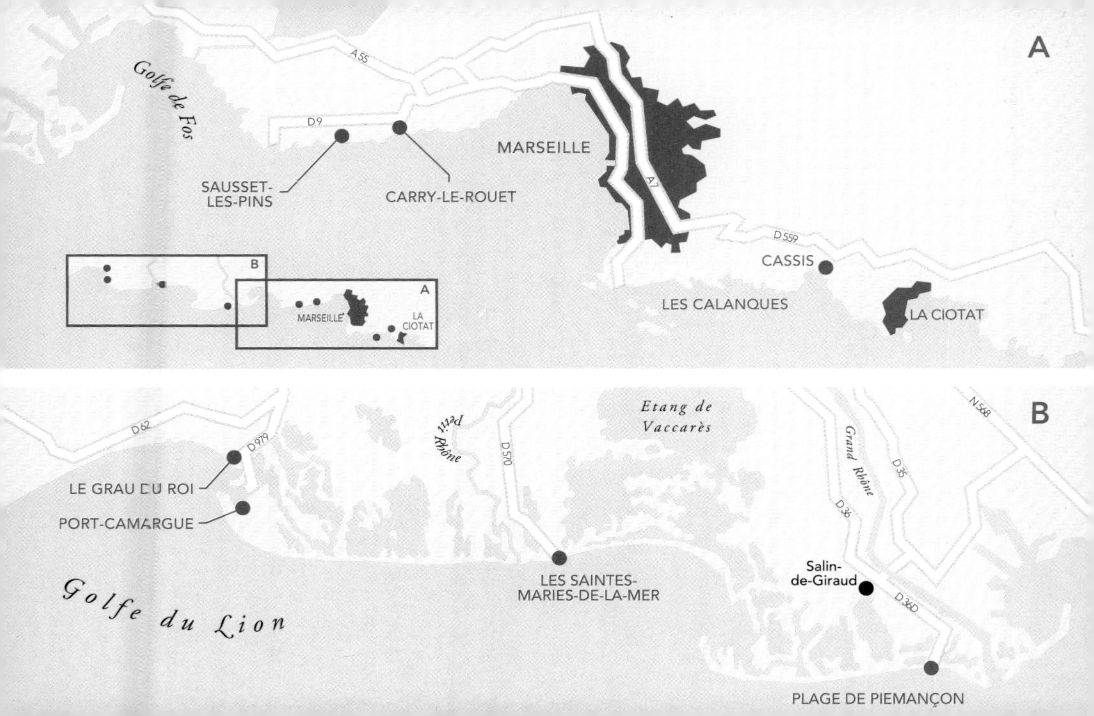
A
Golfe de Fos
A 55
D9
SAUSSET-
LES-PINS
CARRY-LE-ROUET
MARSEILLE
A7
D 559
CASSIS
LES CALANQUES
LA CIOTAT
B
Etang de
Vaccarès
Petit Rhône
D 570
Grand Rhône
D 35
D 36
D 36D
N 568
D 62
D 979
LE GRAU DU ROI
PORT-CAMARGUE
LES SAINTES-
MARIES-DE-LA-MER
Salin-
de-Giraud
PLAGE DE PIEMANÇON
Golfe du Lion

LA CIOTAT 10 km east of Cassis.
This new resort has a good beach to the north of the harbour. See MARSEILLE-EXCURSION 1.

CASSIS 23 km east of Marseille.
An attractive fishing port which is now a fashionable resort with four beaches of shingle: Bestouan, L'Arène, Le Courton and La Grande Mer. See MARSEILLE-EXCURSION 1.

MARSEILLE
There are several good beaches off the Promenade de la Plage: La Corniche, Petit Roucas-Blanc, Grand Roucas-Blanc, Prado and Plage Joseph Vidal.

CARRY-LE-ROUET/SAUSSET-LES-PINS Off the D 49 20 km west of Marseille.
Two fashionable, small resorts with excellent beaches. See MARSEILLE-EXCURSION 2.

PLAGE DE PIEMANÇON On the D 36D south of Salin-de-Giraud.
This is a good, sandy beach lying to the west of the estuary of the Grand Rhône.

LES SAINTES-MARIES-DE-LA-MER
There are 30 km of excellent sandy beaches to both the east and the west of the town.

LE GRAU DU ROI/PORT-CAMARGUE South of Aigues-Mortes.
These 'gone-upmarket' fishing villages to the west of the Camargue have marinas and excellent beaches.

CALANQUES
Deep inlets along the coast between Marseille and Cassis. The best known are Port-Miou, Port-Pin, En Vau, Sugiton and Sormiou. They can be reached by boat from Marseille, Cassis or La Ciotat (see MARSEILLE-EXCURSION 1*) and make excellent family excursions.*

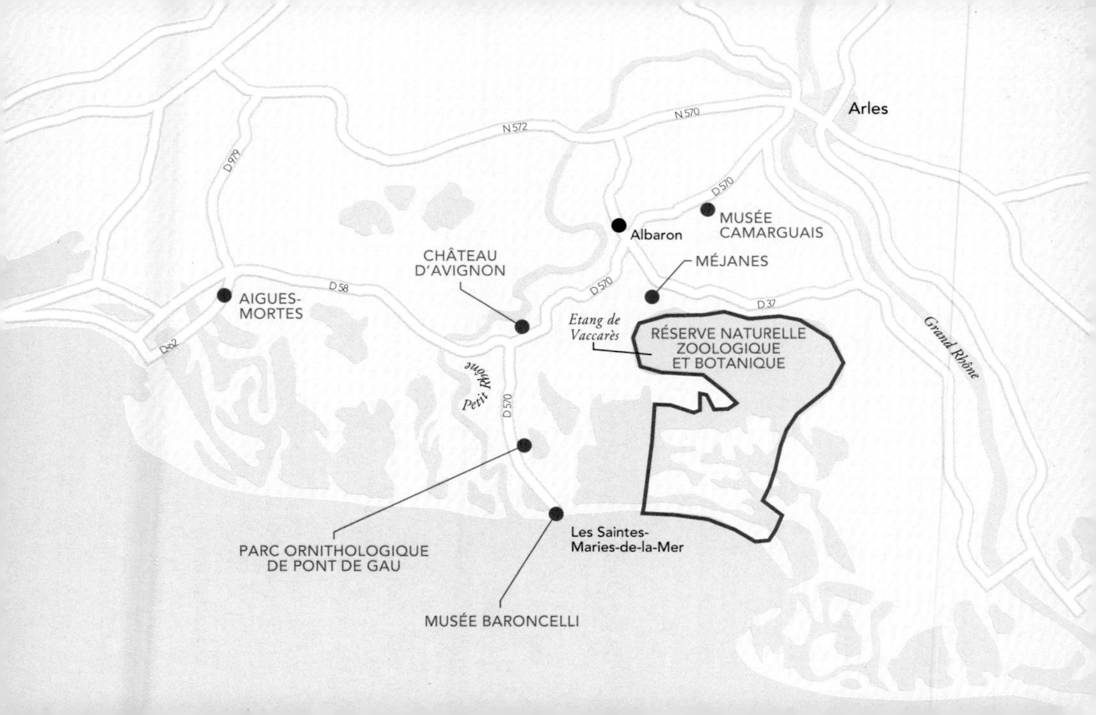
Arles
N 570
N 572
D 979
D 570
MUSÉE
CAMARGUAIS
Albaron
MÉJANES
CHÂTEAU
D'AVIGNON
D 58
AIGUES-
MORTES
D 570
D 37
Etang de
Vaccarès
RÉSERVE NATURELLE
ZOOLOGIQUE
ET BOTANIQUE
Grand Rhône
Petit Rhône
D 570
Les Saintes-
Maries-de-la-Mer
PARC ORNITHOLOGIQUE
DE PONT DE GAU
MUSÉE BARONCELLI

RÉSERVE NATURELLE ZOOLOGIQUE ET BOTANIQUE
South of Étang de Vaccarès.
A permit is required for access to this wildlife reserve which covers 14,000 ha: ask at the Tourist Offices in Arles and Les Saintes-Maries-de-la-Mer, or La Capellière (on the D 36A north of Salin-de-Badon, to the east of the Vaccarès lagoon).

PARC ORNITHOLOGIQUE DE PONT DE GAU
On the D 570, 4 km north of Les Saintes-Maries-de-la-Mer.
❑ 0900-1200, 1400-1900. ❑ 20F.
A series of nature walks allow you to see abundant fauna.

MUSÉE CAMARGUAIS On the D 570 at Pont de Rousty, 20 km north of Les Saintes-Maries-de-la-Mer.
❑ 0900-1200, 1500-1900 Wed.-Mon. ❑ 16F.
An exhibition showing typical Camargue flora, fauna and traditions.

MUSÉE BARONCELLI rue Victor Hugo, in old Hôtel de Ville, Lés Saintes-Maries-de-la-Mer.
❑ 1030-1230, 1400-1800 Wed.-Mon. ❑ 10F.
A display of Camargue paintings, history and furnishings.

MÉJANES AMUSEMENT CENTRE
On the D37 southeast of Albaron.
❑ Prices vary for each activity.
Rodeos, pony and horse trekking, electric railway and horsedrawn carriages: ideal for children.

AIGUES-MORTES On the D 62 to the west of the Camargue.
A beautiful, medieval fortified town, complete with 13thC ramparts and marvellous views. The Tour de Constance should be seen (0900-1200, 1400-1700; 12F). *See* **Aigues-Mortes**.

CHÂTEAU D'AVIGNON 17 km north of Les S.-M.-de-la-Mer.
❑ 0915-1030, 1430-1600. ❑ 21F.
An 18thC chateau with rich furnishings, set in a large park.

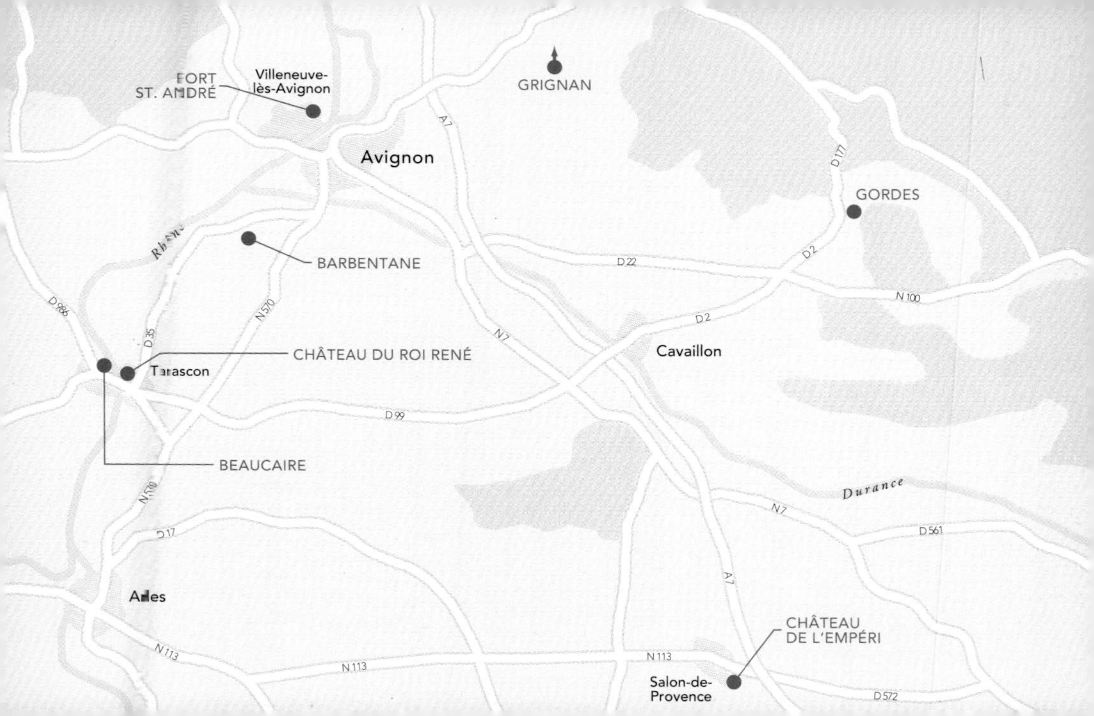

Villeneuve-
lès-Avignon
GRIGNAN
A7
Avignon
D177
GORDES
BARBENTANE
D22
D2
N100
D986
N570
D2
D35
N7
CHÂTEAU DU ROI RENÉ
Cavaillon
D99
BEAUCAIRE
Durance
N7
D17
D561
A7
CHÂTEAU
DE L'EMPÉRI
N113
N113
N113
Salon-de-
Provence
D572

BARBENTANE 10 km southwest of Avignon.
❑ 1000-1200, 1400-1800 Easter-Oct. Sun. only out of season. ❑ 24F.
A handsome 17thC Loire-style chateau, in a small fortified town, decorated with rich Louis XV furnishings. See **AVIGNON-EXCURSION 2**.

BEAUCAIRE 25 km north of Arles.
❑ 1000-1200, 1415-1830 Wed.-Mon. ❑ 10F.
The remains of an 11thC fortress destroyed by Richelieu, on the west bank of the River Rhône facing Tarascon. Visit the Tour de Triangle and the Romanesque chapel.

GORDES 24 km northeast of Cavaillon.
❑ 1000-1200, 1400-1600 Wed.-Mon. ❑ 12F.
Renaissance chateau with machicolated towers overlooking a valley. Now the Vasarély op-art museum. See **AVIGNON-EXCURSION 1**.

GRIGNAN 46 km north of Orange.
❑ 0930-1130, 1430-1730 Wed. pm-Mon. Closed Nov. ❑ 12F.
Renaissance chateau with sumptuous Louis XIII and XIV furnishings. Made famous by Madame de Sévigné's sojourns in the 17thC.

CHÂTEAU DE L'EMPÉRI 35 km northwest of Aix-en-Provence.
❑ 1000-1200, 1430-1830 Wed.-Mon. ❑ 12F.
Mainly 13th-15thC, it was once the residence of the archbishops of Arles. Now houses an army museum. See **AIX-EN-PROVENCE-EXCURSION 1**.

CHÂTEAU DU ROI RENÉ Tarascon, 18 km north of Arles.
❑ 0900-1200, 1400-1700 Wed.-Mon. ❑ 15F.
A 15thC fortress built of golden stone, dominating the town and River Rhône. See the seigneurial apartments, great court, chapels and towers. See **ARLES-EXCURSION**, **René of Anjou**.

FORT ST. ANDRÉ On west bank of River Rhône, facing Avignon.
❑ 0900-1200, 1400-1830 April-Sep.; 1000-1200, 1400-1500 Oct.-Mar.
❑ 11F.
14thC fortress with towers, gateways and 12thC chapel. Great views.

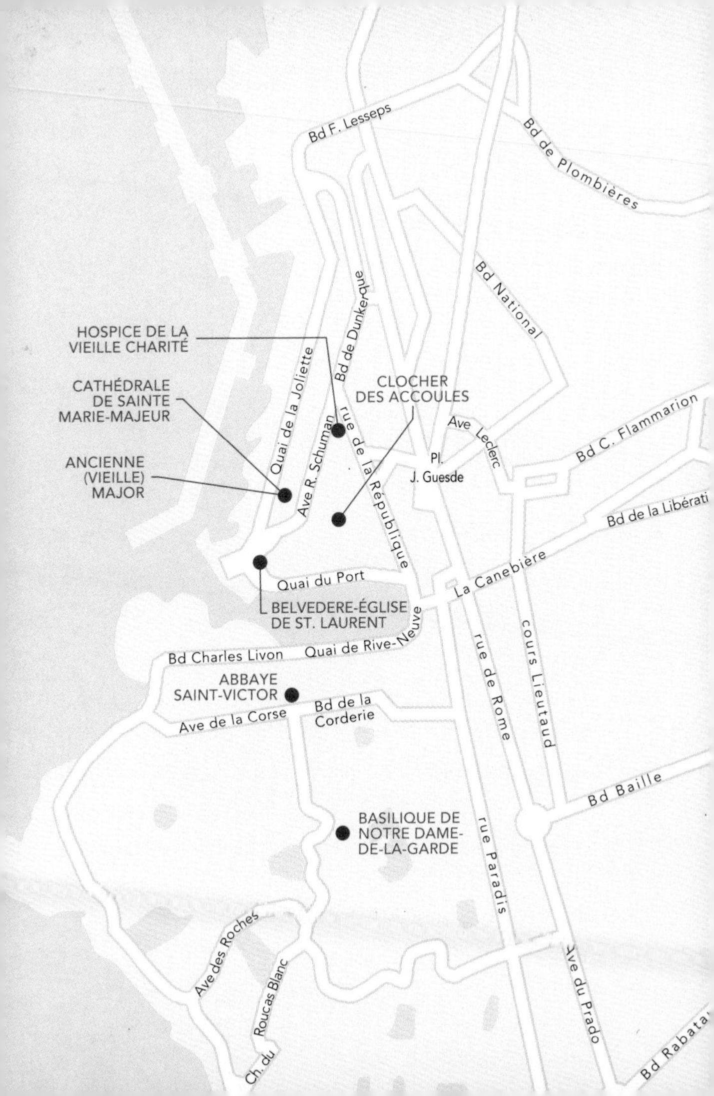
Bd F. Lesseps
Bd de Plombières
Bd National
Bd de Dunkerque
HOSPICE DE LA
VIEILLE CHARITÉ
Quai de la Joliette
CATHÉDRALE
DE SAINTE
MARIE-MAJEUR
CLOCHER
DES ACCOULES
Ave R. Schuman
rue de la République
Ave Leclerc
Bd C. Flammarion
Pl.
J. Guesde
ANCIENNE
(VIEILLE)
MAJOR
Bd de la Libérati
La Canebière
Quai du Port
BELVEDERE-ÉGLISE
DE ST. LAURENT
Quai de Rive-Neuve
Bd Charles Livon
rue de Rome
cours Lieutaud
ABBAYE
SAINT-VICTOR
Bd de la
Corderie
Ave de la Corse
Bd Baille
BASILIQUE DE
NOTRE DAME-
DE-LA-GARDE
rue Paradis
Ave des Roches
Ch. du
Roucas Blanc
Ave du Prado
Bd Rabata

BASILIQUE DE NOTRE DAME-DE-LA-GARDE
Plateaux de la Croix, 7e.
❑ 0730-1900. Bus 60 from cours d'Estienne-d'Orves.
Built in 1864 in Romano-Byzantine style; panoramic views.

ABBAYE SAINT-VICTOR Pl. St-Victor, 7e. West end of Quai de Rive Neuve.
❑ Abbey 0700-1200, 1430-1900. Crypts 1500-1800. ❑ 10F.
5thC building, complete with catacombs. See **Legends & Myths**.

ANCIENNE (VIEILLE) MAJOR Pl. de la Major, 2e. At the west end of the Vieux Port.
❑ 0900-1200, 1400-1700 Wed.-Mon. ❑ 7F.
12thC, Roman provincial-style building; the oldest church in Marseille (no longer in use). See MARSEILLE-WALK.

CATHÉDRALE DE SAINTE-MARIE-MAJEUR
Pl. de la Major, 2e.
❑ 0800-1200, 1430-1900 Tue.-Sun.
An ornate, imposing Romano-Byzantine-style building, constructed in 1853. See MARSEILLE-WALK.

BELVEDERE-ÉGLISE DE ST. LAURENT Parvis St.-Laurent, 2e. Near Fort St. Jean.
Romanesque 12thC church (closed to the public) next to St. Catherine chapel, built in 1604. See MARSEILLE-WALK.

HOSPICE DE LA VIEILLE CHARITÉ rue de la Charité, 2e.
❑ 0900-1200, 1400-1800. M Joliette.
A 17thC building for the town's orphans. See the Puget chapel in the courtyard. See MARSEILLE-WALK.

CLOCHER DES ACCOULÈS Montée des Accoulès, 2e. Near the museums of Vieux Marseille and Docks Romaines.
12thC belfry and church (closed to the public) remains. See MARSEILLE-WALK.

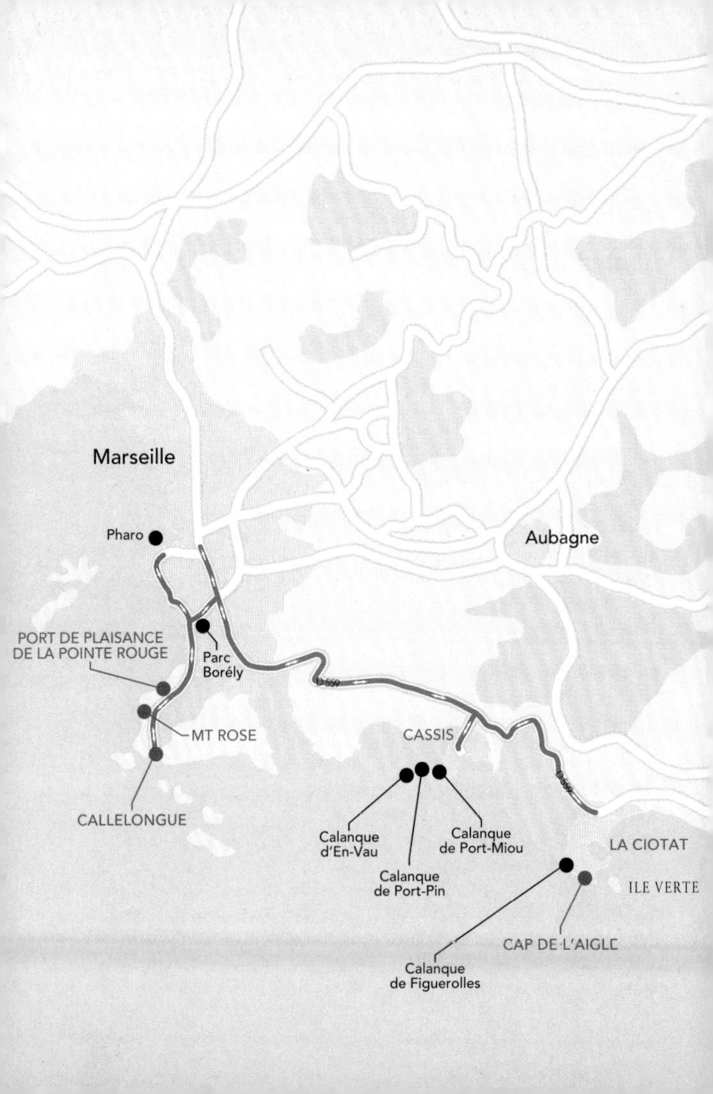
Marseille
Aubagne
Pharo
Parc Borély
PORT DE PLAISANCE DE LA POINTE ROUGE
MT ROSE
CALLELONGUE
D 559
CASSIS
D 559
Calanque d'En-Vau
Calanque de Port-Pin
Calanque de Port-Miou
LA CIOTAT
ILE VERTE
CAP DE L'AIGLE
Calanque de Figuerolles

Excursion 1

A one-day excursion east and southeast to Cassis and La Ciotat.

Take a pleasant 5 km drive along the Corniche President John F. Kennedy beside the Mediterranean from the Pharo (lighthouse) at the western end of the Vieux Port, past various beaches and the race course of the Parc Borély, to the Port de Plaisance de la Pointe Rouge. There are several war memorials commemorating the Allied landings in 1944 and astonishing sea views. If you wish you can continue for 5 km along the coast road past the Prado beach and marina (see **BEACHES**), over the Massif de Marseilleveyre hills and Mt Rose, down to the little harbour of Callelongue, with views of islands, hills and inland villages. Otherwise, head inland for 2 km, turn right on the D 559 and drive for 23 km.
30 km – Cassis. An attractive Riviera-style resort with white villas, fishing port and marina, four beaches (see **BEACHES**) and a casino. Good-quality, dry white wine is grown on the slopes above the town. Try to see the Musée Municipal d'Art et Traditions Populaires in rue X.-d'Authier, (afternoons only Wed. & Thu., Sat. & Sun.). There are boat trips to the *calanques* of En Vau, Port-Pin and Port-Miou (see **BEACHES**) from Quai St. Pierre. The Promenade des Lombards is the main promenade along the seafront, overlooked by the 14thC castle. There are a dozen hotels and good seafood restaurants, including La Plage at Plage du Bestouan, L'Oustau de la Mar on Quai Baux and Nino on Quai Barthélémey. Keep on the D 559 heading east then south for 10 km.
40 km – La Ciotat. A Greek and Roman port, formerly known as Citharista, modern La Ciotat still employs 6000 people in the shipyards (*chantiers navals*) near Cap de l'Aigle. The Vieux Port is attractive, with a large marina and beaches along Bd Beau Rivage (see **BEACHES**). The casino is on the waterfront overlooking the Mediterranean and the Musée Ciotaden is at 51 rue des Poilus (1600-1900 Mon., Wed. & Sat.; 7F). La Ciotat-Plage is the smarter resort with seventeen hotels and several restaurants, notably Provence-Plage, 3 Ave de Provence, and Plaisance, 15 Ave Franklin Roosevelt. You can take local excursions by boat or land to the *calanques* of Mugel and Figuerolles, and Cap de l'Aigle, the eagle's-nest corniche headland, as well as by boat to Ile Verte. Return to Marseille on the D 559.

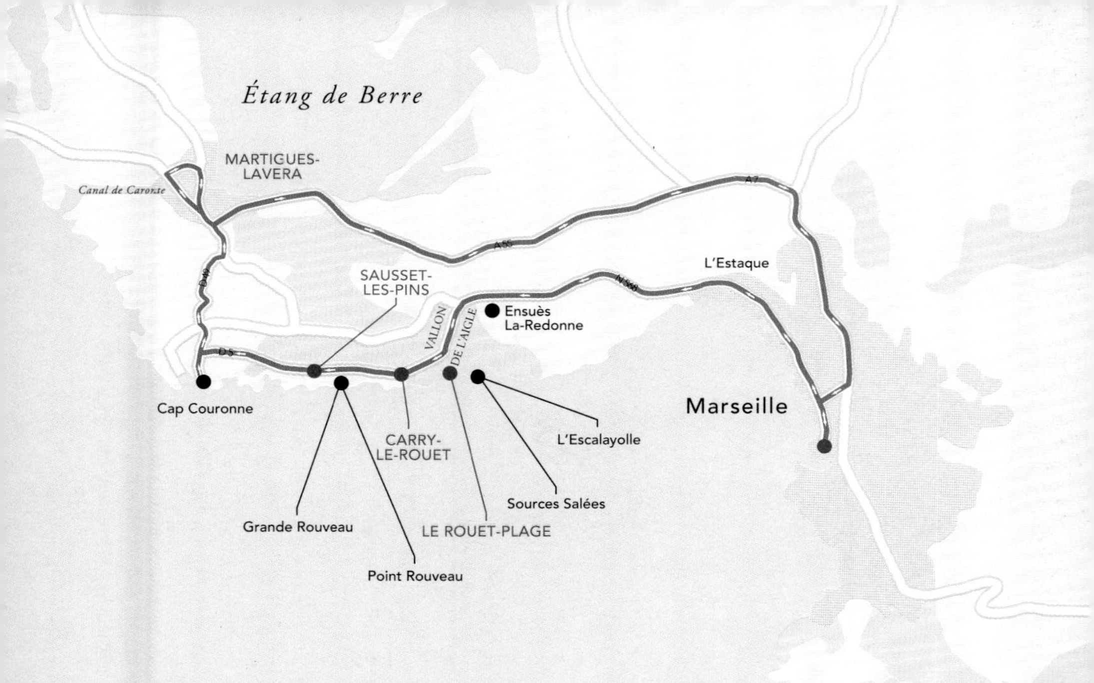

Étang de Berre
MARTIGUES-
LAVERA
Canal de Caronte
A7
A55
D49
D5
N568
SAUSSET-
LES-PINS
VALLON
DE L'AIGLE
L'Estaque
Ensuès
La-Redonne
Cap Couronne
CARRY-
LE-ROUET
Marseille
L'Escalayolle
Sources Salées
Grande Rouveau
LE ROUET-PLAGE
Point Rouveau

Excursion 2

A one-day excursion west and northwest to the beach resorts and calanques *of the Chaîne de l'Esteque and on to Martigues-Lavéra.*

Drive through the docklands due north on the D 5 and N 568 through L'Estaque past several small fishing harbours, then head inland for 4 km and turn west on the D 5 again through Ensuès la-Redonne. Turn left and follow the vallon de l'Aigle south for 3 km, crossing the railway.
27.5 km – Le Rouet-Plage. On the left are the *calanques* of Sources Salées and L'Escalayolle. On your right the D 5 continues into Carry-le-Rouet, a Riviera-style resort with smart villas, woods, a small marina and a beach (see **BEACHES**). There are also hotels and restaurants, of which the Hotel-Restaurant La Tuilière in Ave Draio de la Mar is inexpensive. Follow the D 5 westwards along the coastline for 4 km past two more *calanques*: Grande Rouveau and Point Rouveau.
31.5 km – Sausset-les-Pins (see **BEACHES**). Amid the pine trees is the resort with its fishing village, marina, white villas and two hotels. Continue in the same direction via Cap Couronne for 6 km on the D 49 and then turn inland due north for 12 km.
50 km – Martigues-Lavéra. This curious town is a contrast of ancient and modern. Three fishing villages – Jouquières, Ile Brescou and Ferrières – sit, rather nervously, amid ultra-modern oil complexes at the mouth of the large Étang de Berre (see **A-Z**), which leads, via the Caronte Canal, into the Mediterranean. Definitely worth visiting is the much-painted fishermen's wharf called the 'Birds' looking-glass'. You should also visit the Felix Ziem museum with its many Provençal works (1000-1200, 1430-1830 Wed.-Sun.; 10F); the Canal Saint-Sebastien; and the Église de Ste-Madeleine-de-L'Ile on Ile Brescou. There are excellent views from the Pont St. Sebastien. You can eat out in style at the Hotel-Grill Campanile in Bd Tholon. In late June there are fireworks, concerts and a water-jousting competition, and in early July a nocturnal boat procession.
Return to Marseille along the A 55 and the A7 (40 km).

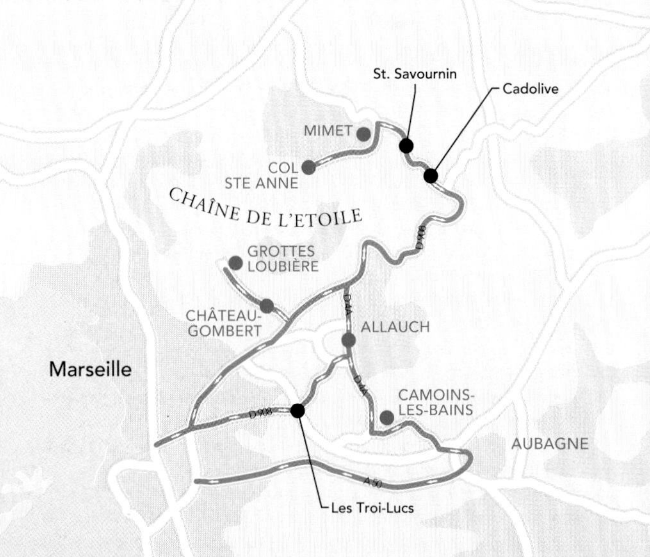

Cassis

La Ciotat

Excursion 3

A half-day excursion to Allauch, then from there to: either the villages to the east of the Chaîne de l'Etoile mountain range; or the home of the French Foreign Legion at Aubagne; or Château-Gombert and the Grottes Loubière.

Leave Marseille via La Canebière and drive for 2 km, keeping the Jardin Zoologique on your left, then drive for another 11 km on Bl. la Blancarde (signposted for Les Troi-Lucs).

13 km – Allauch. Stop to look back at Marseille and the Vieux Port from the grounds of the 11thC castle. Visit the 16thC church of Notre Dame du Château and the Musée du Vieil Allauch, 11 Pl. Bellot (Wed., Sat. & Sun. pm; 6F). From Allauch you have several options.

Either: continue north on the D 4A and then the D 908 on the east side of the Chaîne de l'Etoile mountain range to the villages of Cadolive, St. Savournin, and Mimet (from where there are great views). Then either by car or on foot climb up the Col Ste Anne. This is an ideal spot for a picnic. Return on the same route to Allauch and thence retrace your steps back to Marseille.

Or: go southeast on the D 4A via the small spa resort of Camoins-les-Bains under the A 50 into Aubagne (pop: 38,000), the birth place of Marcel Pagnol (1895-1974), novelist and film-maker. This is also the home of the French Foreign Legion. Since Algerian independence these tough, well-trained soldiers of all nationalities – shades of *Beau Geste* – have been based in Aubagne. Boys of all ages will enjoy a visit to the museum to see their battle honours, flags, weapons, paintings, prints and Legion memorabilia (1000-1200, 1500-1900 Wed., Sat. & Sun.; 22F). You can return to Marseille on the A 50 (36 km).

Or: continue for 4 km northwest on the D 44F to Château-Gombert, which has a 17thC church and a local folklore museum with displays of costumes, furniture, glass and pottery (1500-1900 Mon., Sat. & Sun.; 12F). An International Festival of Folklore takes place during the first two weeks of July. Now continue for 3 km northwest to the Grottes Loubière: the five caves are filled with stalactites and stalagmites for 1500 m (0900-1200, 1400-1730 Wed.-Mon.; guided tour 20F). Return via Château-Gombert, the D 44 and the D 908 southwest to Marseille.

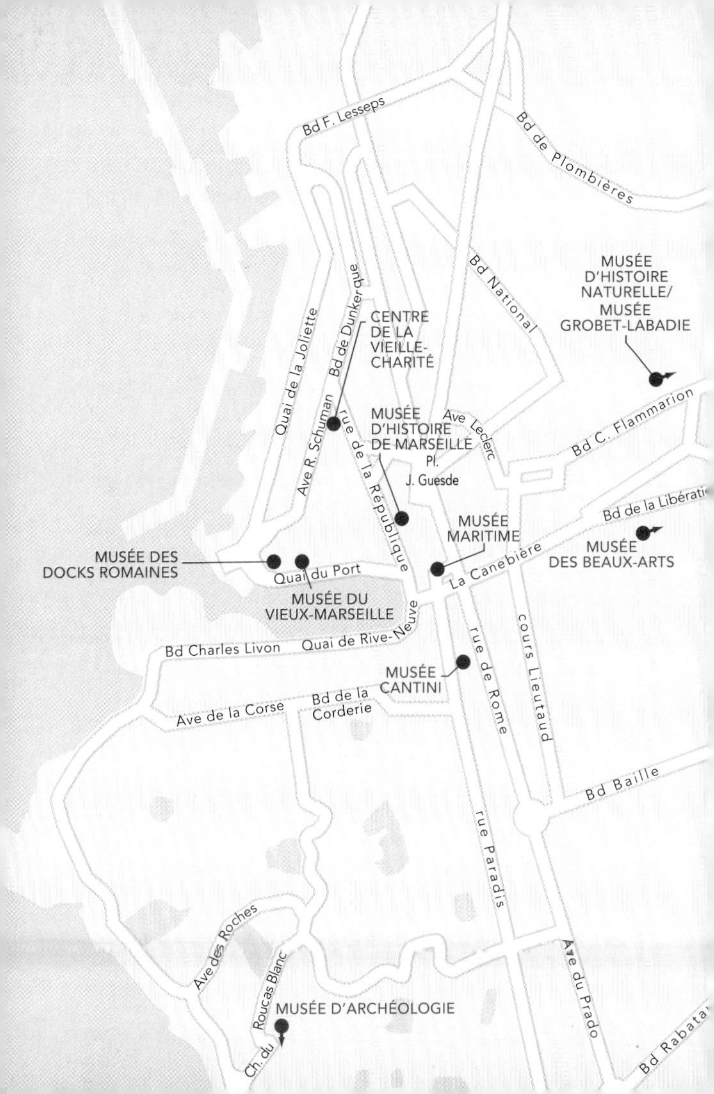
Bd F. Lesseps
Bd de Plombières
Bd National
MUSÉE
D'HISTOIRE
NATURELLE/
MUSÉE
GROBET-LABADIE
CENTRE
DE LA
VIEILLE-
CHARITÉ
Quai de la Joliette
Bd de Dunkerque
Ave R. Schuman
rue de la République
MUSÉE
D'HISTOIRE
DE MARSEILLE
Ave Leclerc
Pl.
J. Guesde
Bd C. Flammarion
Bd de la Libérati
MUSÉE
MARITIME
MUSÉE
DES BEAUX-ARTS
MUSÉE DES
DOCKS ROMAINES
Quai du Port
La Canebière
MUSÉE DU
VIEUX-MARSEILLE
Bd Charles Livon
Quai de Rive-Neuve
rue de Rome
cours Lieutaud
MUSÉE
CANTINI
Ave de la Corse
Bd de la
Corderie
Bd Baille
rue Paradis
Ave des Roches
Ave du Prado
Ch. du Roucas Blanc
MUSÉE D'ARCHÉOLOGIE
Bd Rabata

MUSÉE GROBET-LABADIÈ 140 Bd Longchamp, 4e.
❑ 1000-1200, 1400-1830 Wed. pm-Mon. M Cinq Avenue. ❑ 8F.
A mixed bag of medieval sculpture, faïence, Italian primitifs, *musical instruments, 19thC paintings and armour.*

MUSÉE DES BEAUX-ARTS Palais Longchamp, 4e.
❑ 1000-1200, 1400-1815 Wed. pm-Mon. M Cinq Avenue. ❑ 8F.
The 19thC palace has a collection of works by Provençaux painters, as well as by Dufy, Ingres, David and Rubens, and local caricaturist Honoré Daumier (1808-79).

MUSÉE D'HISTOIRE DE MARSEILLE Centre Bourse, 1e, on the north side of the Vieux Port.
❑ 1000-1900 Tue.-Sat. ❑ 8F.
Traces the history of the town from the 6thC. Situated in the Jardin des Vestiges. *See* MARSEILLE-WALK.

MUSÉE DU VIEUX-MARSEILLE rue de la Prison, on the north side of the Vieux Port.
❑ 1000-1200, 1400-1800 Wed. pm-Mon. ❑ 8F (free Sun. am).
The building has a remarkable facade and is known as 'Maison Diamantée'. Inside there are reconstructions of various scenes from Provençal life. *See* MARSEILLE-WALK.

MUSÉE CANTINI 19 rue Grignan, 6e.
❑ 1000-1200, 1400-1900 Wed. pm-Mon. M Castellane. ❑ 8F.
The Marseille sculptor gifted this 17thC house to the city. It contains 600 pieces of 18thC faïence and 400 contemporary paintings, as well as carpets, Renaissance furniture and Greek pottery.

MUSÉE DES DOCKS ROMAINES Pl. Vivaux, on the north side of the Vieux Port.
❑ 1000-1200, 1400-1830 Wed. pm-Mon. ❑ 9F.
Trading exhibits and maritime displays of the Roman era. The museum is located on the docks' original site. *See* MARSEILLE-WALK.

Vieille-Charité

MUSÉE D'ARCHÉOLOGIE Parc Borély, 8e.
❑ 0930-1200, 1300-1730 Wed.-Mon. M Prado. ❑ 8F.
Greek, Gallo-Roman and Egyptian antiques displayed in this museum located in the lovely Borély gardens. *See* **MARSEILLE-WHAT TO SEE.**

CENTRE DE LA VIEILLE-CHARITÉ rue de la Charité, 2e.
❑ 1000-1200, 1400-1700 Wed.-Mon. M Joliette. ❑ 8F.
Built by Pierre Puget, a leading 19thC Marseille architect, the galleries house an Egyptian collection and another collection of material commemorating Revolutionary Marseille. *See* **MARSEILLE-WALK.**

MUSÉE MARITIME Off La Canebière, near Pl. Gen. de Gaulle.
❑ 1000-1200, 1400-1630 Wed.-Mon. ❑ 12F.
A huge building (built in 1852) with displays of maps, paintings, models of ships, docks and trade activities of the port of Marseille since the days of the Greek and Roman traders. It is housed in the old Palais de la Bourse.

MUSÉE D'HISTOIRE NATURELLE Palais Longchamp, 4e.
❑ 1000-1200, 1400-1630 Wed. pm-Mon. M Cinq Avenue. ❑ 6F.
Regional prehistory, mineralogical and zoological collections.

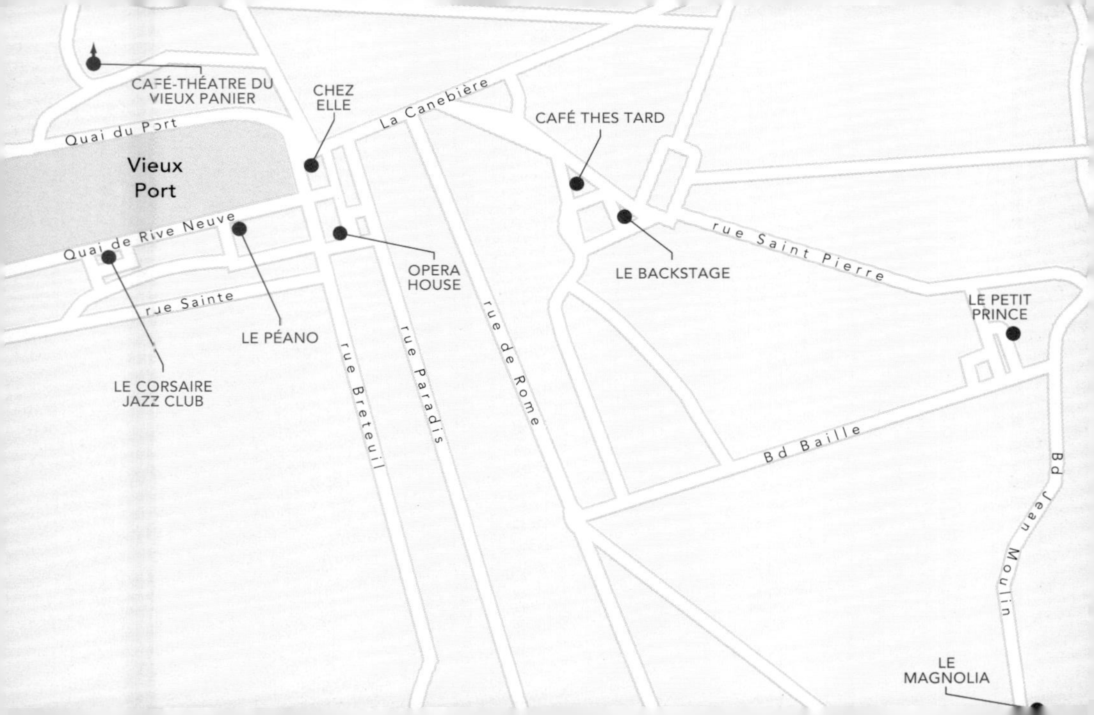

CAFÉ-THÉATRE DU VIEUX PANIER
CHEZ ELLE
La Canebière
CAFÉ THES TARD
Quai du Port
Vieux Port
Quai de Rive Neuve
OPERA HOUSE
LE BACKSTAGE
rue Saint Pierre
rue Sainte
LE PÉANO
LE PETIT PRINCE
LE CORSAIRE JAZZ CLUB
rue Breteuil
rue Paradis
rue de Rome
Bd Baille
Bd Jean Moulin
LE MAGNOLIA

L'OPÉRA (Municipal Opera House) Pl. Reyer/2 rue Molière, 1e, 250 m south of the Tourist Office.
A year-long programme of opera, ballet and theatre.

CAFÉ-THÉATRE DU VIEUX PANIER 50-2 rue Sainte-Françoise, 2e, near Ancienne Major.
Dinner with cabaret, dancing girls and burlesque, followed by a discotheque Thu.-Sat.

LE BACKSTAGE 2 rue André Poggioli, 6e.
❑ 1200-1400 & every evening. M Notre Dame du Mont Cours Julien.
Café-theatre-restaurant with rock concerts. On Sunday afternoons you can hear the singers 'Théatre de la Niche'.

CAFÉ THÈS TARD 2 rue Vian, 6e.
❑ 2100-late. M Notre Dame du Mont Cours Julien.
Café and dinner-cabaret; there is also an exhibition gallery.

LE PETIT PRINCE 8 rue Bravet, 5e.
M 1 km east of Notre Dame du Mont Cours Julien.
Dine while local actors tell local jokes in argot.

LE CORSAIRE JAZZ CLUB 40 rue Plan Fourmiguier.
❑ 2100-late. Bus 23, 45.
Smoky atmospheric club with modern and Trad jazz.

CHEZ ELLE 13 rue Beauvau, 1e. Behind the Tourist Office.
Traditional cabaret-bar, with topical humour in argot.

LE PÉANO 30 cours d'Estienne d'Orves, 1e.
Bus 23, 45. M Quai de Rive Neuve.
A typical piano-bar, featuring jazz musicians.

LE MAGNOLIA 145 rue Rabatau, 8e.
M 1 km east of Perier.
This is a rather smart cabaret-piano bar.

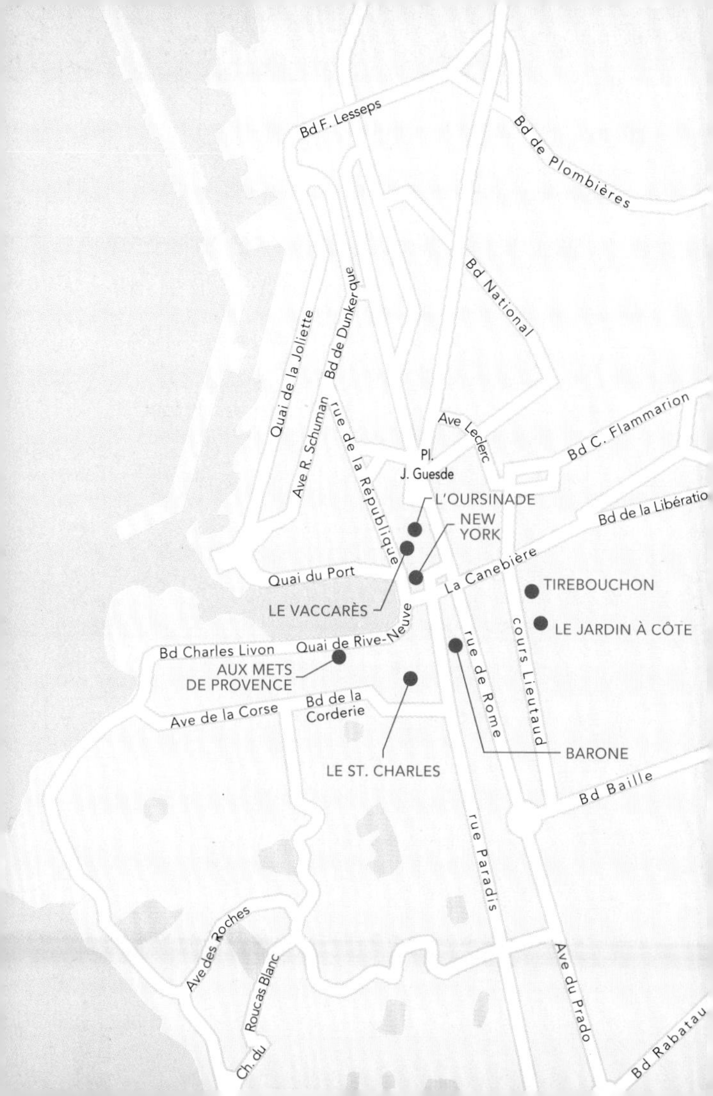

Bd F. Lesseps
Bd de Plombières
Bd National
Quai de la Joliette
Bd de Dunkerque
Ave R. Schuman
rue de la République
Ave Leclerc
Bd C. Flammarion
Pl.
J. Guesde
L'OURSINADE
NEW
YORK
Bd de la Libératio
Quai du Port
La Canebière
TIREBOUCHON
LE VACCARÈS
cours Lieutaud
LE JARDIN À CÔTE
Quai de Rive-Neuve
Bd Charles Livon
rue de Rome
AUX METS
DE PROVENCE
Bd de la
Corderie
Ave de la Corse
BARONE
LE ST. CHARLES
Bd Baille
rue Paradis
Ave des Roches
Roucas Blanc
Ch. du
Ave du Prado
Bd Rabatau

L'OURSINADE Hôtel Frantel, rue Neuve St. Martin, 1e.
❑ 1200-1430, 1930-2230 Mon.-Sat. Closed Aug. M Colbert.
❑ Expensive.
Oursinade *fish soup,* cuisine Provençale *and views of Greek ruins.*

AUX METS DE PROVENCE 18 Quai Rive-Neuve.
❑ 1245-1430, 2000-2130 Tue.-Sat. Bus 23, 45. ❑ Expensive.
Idiosyncratic, brilliant restauranteur; try the boeuf en daube.

NEW YORK 7 Quai des Belges.
❑ 1230-1430, 2000-2230 Mon.-Sat. M Vieux Port. ❑ Expensive.
Classic fish restaurant – very popular – with views of the harbour.

LE ST. CHARLES Hôtel Le St. Charles, 26 rue Breteuil, 6e.
❑ 1200-1400, 1900-2100 Mon.-Sat. M Estrangin Préfecture.
❑ Moderate.
Try the couscous. *The prix fixe menu is good value.*

TIREBOUCHON 11 cours Julien, 6e.
❑ 1230-1430, 2000-2230 Tue.-Sat. Closed July & Aug. M Notre Dame du Mont Cours Julien. ❑ Moderate.
A family-run bistro with good local wines.

LE JARDIN À CÔTÉ 65 cours Julien, 6e.
❑ 1200-1430, 2000-0100 Mon.-Sat. M Notre Dame du Mont Cours Julien. ❑ Inexpensive.
Eat inside or out. The plat du jour *is good value, as are the salads.*

LE VACCARÈS 64 rue de la République, 1e.
❑ 1130-1300, 1930-2400 Mon.-Sat. M Colbert. ❑ Inexpensive.
Friendly ambience, ample portions and tasty lamb dishes.

BARONE 43 rue Vacon.
❑ 1200-1430, 1900-2145 Tue.-Sun. Closed July & Aug. M Vieux Port.
❑ Inexpensive.
All the shellfish and bouillabaisse dishes are good value.

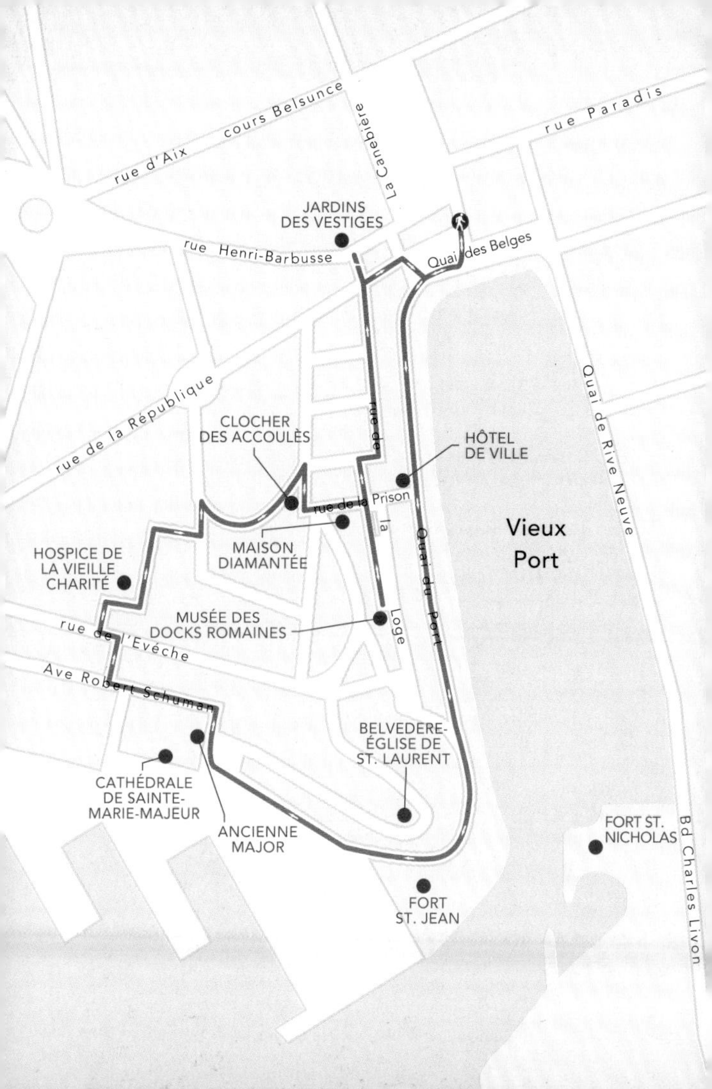
rue d'Aix
cours Belsunce
La Canebière
rue Paradis
JARDINS DES VESTIGES
rue Henri-Barbusse
Quai des Belges
rue de la République
CLOCHER DES ACCOULÈS
rue de la Loge
HÔTEL DE VILLE
rue de la Prison
MAISON DIAMANTÉE
Quai du Port
Vieux Port
Quai de Rive Neuve
HOSPICE DE LA VIEILLE CHARITÉ
MUSÉE DES DOCKS ROMAINES
rue de l'Evéche
Ave Robert Schuman
BELVEDERE-ÉGLISE DE ST. LAURENT
CATHÉDRALE DE SAINTE-MARIE-MAJEUR
ANCIENNE MAJOR
FORT ST. NICHOLAS
Bd Charles Livon
FORT ST. JEAN

2 hr.
Start at the Tourist Office in La Canebière (see **MARSEILLE-WHAT TO SEE**). Turn left into the Quai des Belges facing the picturesque Vieux Port 1 km in length and 300 m across. It is full of yachts and fishing boats, and, at the sea end, ferry boats scuttle across the harbour mouth. Each morning the freshly caught fish is marketed and there is fierce competition between restauranteurs and housewives planning their lunch. Turn right along the Quai du Port (i.e. the north side) with its numerous restaurants and cafés. Soon you will see Mansard's 17thC Hôtel de Ville (town hall) for which Pierre Puget, the notable local architect and sculptor, designed a magnificent medallion (see **MARSEILLE-WHAT TO SEE**). At the end of the Quai notice the 12thC Belvedere-Église de St. Laurent (see **MARSEILLE-CHURCHES**), the Musée des Docks Romaines (see **MARSEILLE-MUSEUMS 1**) and the two forts (St. Jean and St. Nicholas) guarding the entrance to the harbour. There is a road tunnel under the harbour and ferry boats sail between the Hôtel de Ville and the Pl. aux Huiles (4F per crossing).
Now turn inland and head north towards the two Cathedrals, the old and the new, rather incongruously near the modern docks and Gare Maritime. The huge newer building with cupolas and striped stonework

was constructed in 1853 by Vaudoyer in Romano-Byzantine style, and is sumptuously decorated inside (see **MARSEILLE-CHURCHES**). Nestling by its side is the beautiful little 12thC Romanesque Ancienne Major (see **MARSEILLE-CHURCHES**). Although needlessly truncated when the new Cathedral was built, the inside should be seen. Two altars, one of 1122, the other 15thC, and Della Robbia porcelain bas-relief should be noted. The building is no longer used as a church.
Head inland and walk east across the busy Ave Robert Schumann for 250 m through the Pl. Francis Chivat towards the large Italianate-style Hospice de la Vieille Charité, now restored to its 17thC purity. The three-tiered arcaded buildings were built to house orphans and the town's mendicants but are now an exhibition and conference centre. In the central courtyard is the handsome chapel built by Pierre Puget with its imposing cupola (see **MARSEILLE-CHURCHES, MUSEUMS 2**).
Now stroll towards the Vieux Port down the narrow winding streets to the 12thC Clocher des Accoulès near the Hôtel-Dieu gardens. No. 2 rue de la Prison is the unusual 16thC 'Maison Diamantée' with its lus-

Hôtel de Ville

trous faceted facade. Inside is the Musée du Vieux-Marseille (see **MARSEILLE-MUSEUMS 1**). An eclectic collection includes Provençal *santons* (see **A-Z**), furniture, porcelain, playing cards, maps and paintings of Marseille life through the centuries. Take a short detour 200 m west along the rue de la Loge to the Pl. Vivaux where the Musée des Docks Romaines is situated. It has a wide range of Greek and Roman trading and mercantile artefacts (storage jars, anchors, ships' stays and maps) all displayed on the site where they were used 2500 years ago (see **MARSEILLE-MUSEUMS 1**).
Retrace your steps inland and head east, parallel to the Quai de Port, behind the Hôtel de Ville for 500 m to the Jardins des Vestiges which contain the town ramparts and the Musée des Vestiges/D'Histoire de Marseille. The museum is a collection of Greek quays, towers and reservoirs set amid lawns – all quite fascinating (see **MARSEILLE-MUSEUMS 1**). Return from the rue Henri-Barbusse towards the Quai des Belges and the Tourist Office.

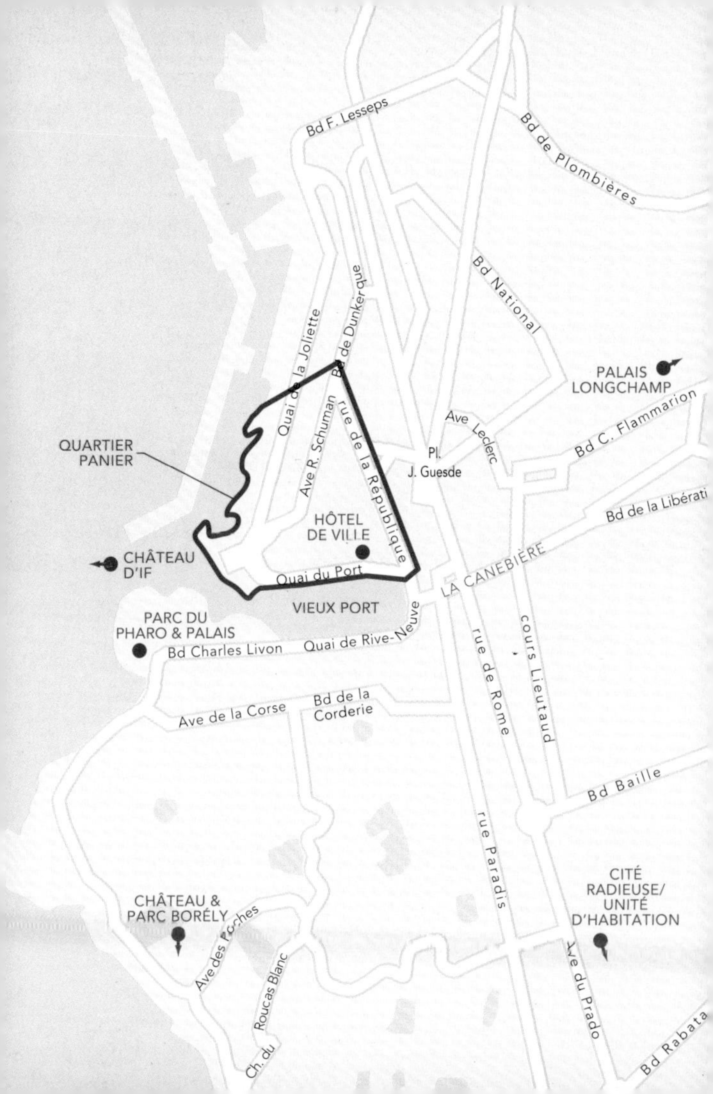

Bd F. Lesseps
Bd de Plombières
Bd National
Quai de la Joliette
Bd de Dunkerque
Ave R. Schuman
rue de la République
PALAIS LONGCHAMP
Ave Leclerc
Bd C. Flammarion
Pl. J. Guesde
QUARTIER PANIER
HÔTEL DE VILLE
Bd de la Libérati
CHÂTEAU D'IF
Quai du Port
LA CANEBIÈRE
VIEUX PORT
PARC DU PHARO & PALAIS
Bd Charles Livon
Quai de Rive-Neuve
rue de Rome
cours Lieutaud
Ave de la Corse
Bd de la Corderie
Bd Baille
rue Paradis
CITÉ RADIEUSE/ UNITÉ D'HABITATION
CHÂTEAU & PARC BORÉLY
Ave des Roches
Ch. du Roucas Blanc
Ave du Prado
Bd Rabata

VIEUX PORT West end of La Canebière.
The heart of Marseille, full of yachts and ferries, and surrounded by old buildings, including the Hôtel de Ville and many good restaurants. Try to visit one of the morning fish markets. See **MARSEILLE-WALK.**

LA CANEBIÈRE
Long, famous, noisy but rather sleazy main street leading from the Vieux Port east for 1 km; full of shops, cafés and hotels, and morning flower markets. See **MARSEILLE-WALK.**

CHÂTEAU D'IF 3 km southeast, offshore.
❑ 0830-1200, 1330-2000 June-Sep.; 1000-1600 Oct.-May. ❑ Round trip 36F from Quai des Belges.
Castle built by Francis I in 1524 on a rocky island. Visit the prison where Dumas' Comte de Monte Cristo was imprisoned. There are panoramic views from the chapel terrace. See **Boat Cruises**.

CHÂTEAU & PARC BORÉLY Ave Clot-Bey, east of the Vieux Port.
❑ 1000-1700 Wed. pm-Mon. M Rd Point du Prado, then walk.
Elegant 18thC chateau in large park with lake. See **MARSEILLE-MUSEUMS 2.**

PALAIS LONGCHAMP 600 m east of La Canebière.
❑ 0930-1200, 1300-1730 Wed.-Mon. M Cinq Avenue.
Baroque palace, water tower and gardens. See **MARSEILLE-MUSEUMS 1 & 2.**

HÔTEL DE VILLE & QUARTIER PANIER Off Quai du Port.
The historic old town spreads inland from the 17thC Hôtel de Ville. See **MARSEILLE-WALK.**

PARC DU PHARO & PALAIS West end of the Vieux Port.
19thC pink building (closed). The park has good views of the city.

CITÉ RADIEUSE/UNITÉ D'HABITATION Bd Michelet.
M Rd Point du Prado.
In 1952 this concrete jungle made news in the world of international architecture. See **Le Corbusier.**

Villeneuve-lès-Avignon
Avignon
A7
ABBAYE DE SÉNANQUE
D177
Rhône
D22
D2
N100
D986
N570
ABBAYE DE ST. MICHEL-DE-FRIGOLET
N7
Cavaillon
D35
Tarascon
D99
ABBAYE DE ST. ROMAN
Durance
N7
D17
D561
ABBAYE DE MONTMAJOUR
ABBAYE DE SILVACANE
Arles
N113
Salon-de-Provence

ABBAYE DE MONTMAJOUR On the D 17, 7 km northeast of the town of Arles.
❑ 0900-1200, 1400-1800 Wed.-Mon. Closed Nov. ❑ 17F.
A formidable 10thC Benedictine Abbey, situated on a hill, which at one time attracted 100,000 pilgrims every year. There is a 14thC keep and a charming cloister with a well and animal carvings. See ARLES-EXCURSION.

ABBAYE DE SÉNANQUE On D 177, 7 km northwest of Gordes.
❑ 1000-1200, 1400-1800. ❑ 20F.
12thC Cistercian Abbey set amid lovely lavender beds in a peaceful valley. Now a curious mixture of lay and cultural activity, including the Toureg museum, Institute for Medieval Studies, and summer concerts, exhibitions and lecture courses. See AVIGNON-EXCURSION 1, **Petrarch**.

ABBAYE DE SILVACANE On the D 561, 28 km north of Aix-en-Provence.
❑ 1000-1145, 1400-1845 Thu.-Mon. ❑ 12F.
Well-restored abbey built by the Cistercian Order in 1144. There is a chapterhouse, a refectory and a cloister.

ABBAYE DE ST. MICHEL-DE-FRIGOLET On the D 35, 15 km southwest of Avignon.
❑ 0900-1800. ❑ Free; offertory welcome.
Originally founded in the 10thC by the monks of Montmajour, this handsome abbey complex, in its quiet valley setting, with church, 11thC chapel, cloister, pilgrim hostel and small museum, is still in active use. Visitors are always welcome at the services to hear the fine singing. See AVIGNON-EXCURSION 2.

ABBAYE DE ST. ROMAN Off the D 986, 5 km northwest of Beaucaire and Tarascon.
❑ 1000-1900 Fri.-Wed. (July-Oct.); 1500-1800 Nov.-June. ❑ 10F.
This building was originally a 12thC abbey, then a fortress, then a castle, but was finally dismantled in 1850. It is now undergoing extensive restoration. See St. Romanus' tomb, the Lanterne des Mortes, the monks' cells and the large hall.

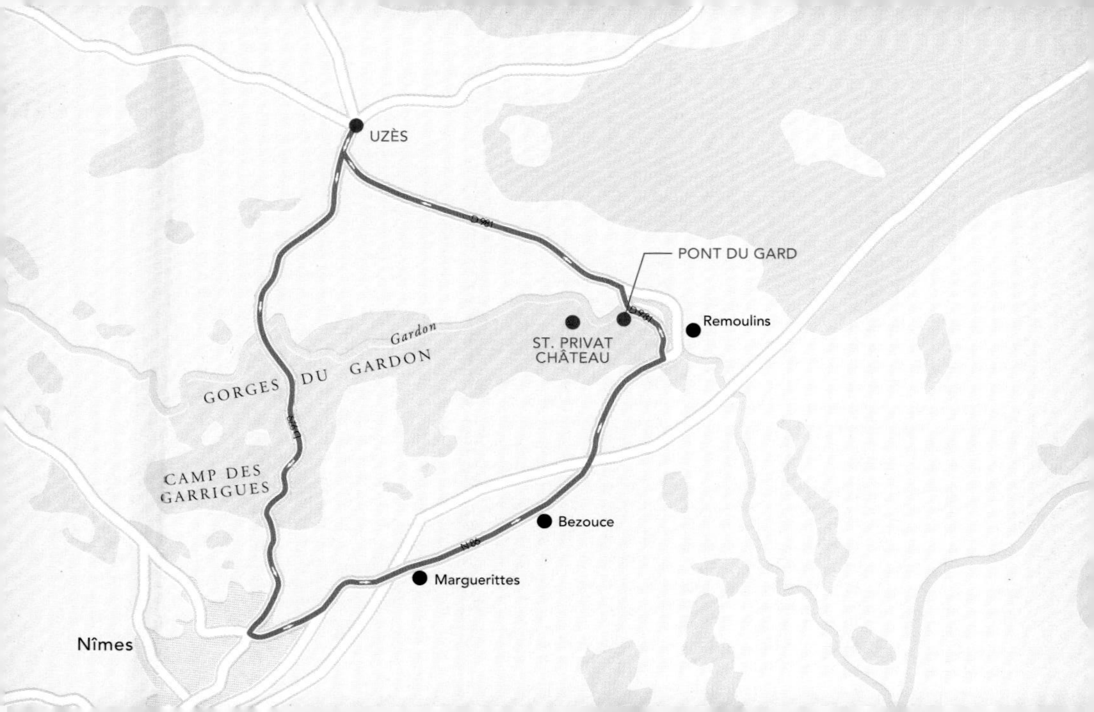
UZÈS
D981
PONT DU GARD
D981
Remoulins
ST. PRIVAT
CHÂTEAU
Gardon
GORGES DU GARDON
D979
CAMP DES
GARRIGUES
Bezouce
N86
Marguerittes
Nîmes

Excursion

A one-day excursion to Pont du Gard and Uzès.

Drive northeast on the N 86 for 23 km via Marguerittes and Bezouce, over and under the A 9 to Remoulins amid cherry and fruit orchards. Then go 3 km west on the D 981 parallel to the River Gardon.
26 km – Pont du Gard. Park your car in one of two parking areas (fee payable). A covered canal was built in 19 BC by the Romans to bring pure water from the River Eure via the Pont du Gard (see **A-Z**) to the Castellum in the north of Nîmes, a distance of 40 km (see **NÎMES-WHAT TO SEE 1**). Napoleon III had the structure repaired. The bridge has three tiers spanning the River Gardon: six arches in the bottom tier; 11 arches in the middle and finally the top level, the covered canal with 35 arches. The aqueduct is 275 m across and the modern road passes underneath it. You can walk across the top, preferably not in a wind, taking sensible precautions. The St. Privat Château lies 2.5 km west, on the banks of the river, and there are two moderately-priced restaurants on the D 981 with views of the Pont du Gard. This is also an excellent site for a picnic and, if you feel active, canoes can be rented locally.
Continue for 19 km west on the D 981.
42 km – Uzès (pop: 8000) is an attractive medieval town. The Ducal Palace (*Duché*), owned by the royal family of Crussol d'Uzès for a thousand years, has a Renaissance facade, Louis XV salon, three towers, a 16thC chapel and the 11thC Bermonde square (0930-1200, 1430-1830 Tue.-Sun.; 32F). Also worth visiting are the Pl. aux Herbes, the Église de St. Etienne, Maison Dampmartin, the old Mint, the 4thC Crypt, the 17thC Cathédrale de St. Théodorit (note especially the organ). Above all don't miss the towers of Fenestrelle, Bermonde, Du Roi, Evêques and Vicomte. The town's restaurants include the rather expensive Entraigues in Pl. Evêché, and the inexpensive La Taverne at 4 rue Sigalon. Summer festivals in the town include Nuits Musicales d'Uzès in the second half of July and the *fête votive* at the beginning of August, when bulls run through the streets and wine and *pastis* flow in abundance.
Return the 25 km to Nîmes on the D 979, a winding road which runs through the Gorges du Gardon and the Guarrigues hills.

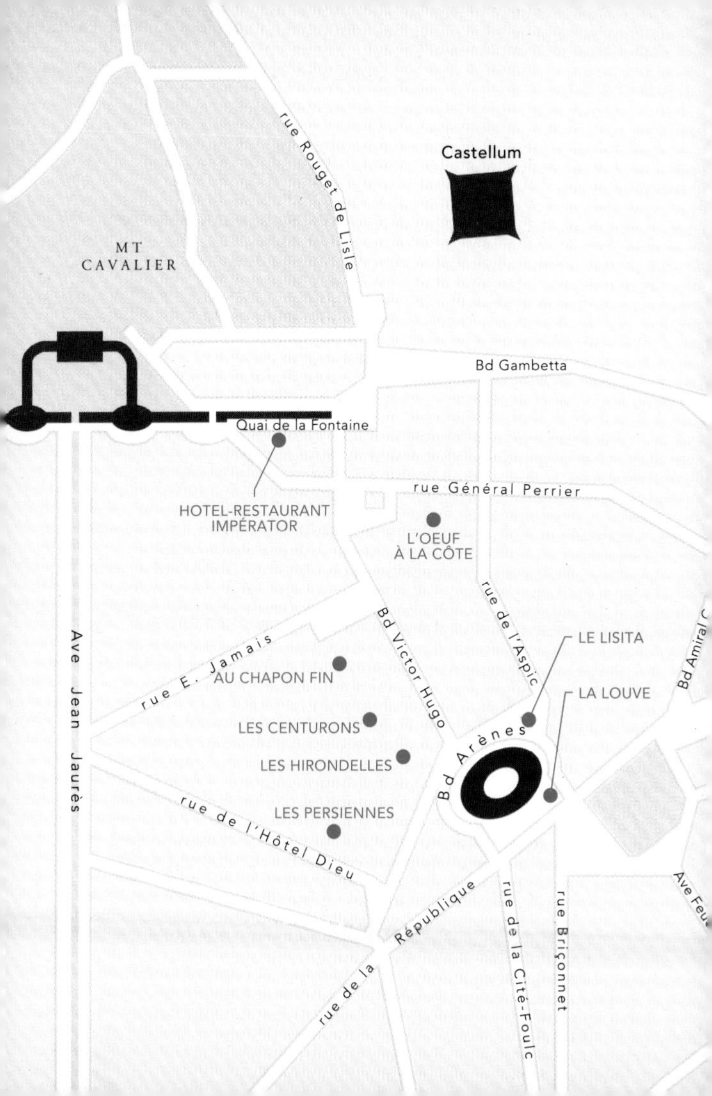

Castellum

rue Rouget de Lisle

MT
CAVALIER

Bd Gambetta

Quai de la Fontaine

HOTEL-RESTAURANT
IMPÉRATOR

rue Général Perrier

L'OEUF
À LA CÔTE

rue de l'Aspic

Bd Victor Hugo

rue E. Jamais

AU CHAPON FIN

LE LISITA

LA LOUVE

Bd Amiral

LES CENTURONS

Bd Arènes

LES HIRONDELLES

Ave Jean Jaurès

rue de l'Hôtel Dieu

LES PERSIENNES

rue de la République

rue de la Cité-Foulc

rue Briçonnet

Ave Feu

HOTEL-RESTAURANT IMPÉRATOR Quai de la Fontaine.
❑ 1200-1400, 1930-2100, except Sat. lunch. Closed Feb.
❑ Expensive.
Classic Provençal cuisine served on a lovely terrace; try the Brandade de Morue.

LE LISITA 2 Bd Arènes.
❑ 1200-1430, 2000-2200 Sun.-Fri. Closed Aug. ❑ Expensive.
Good regional cooking; ask for tournedos Mistral.

LA LOUVE 1 rue de la République.
❑ 1200-1500, 1930-2100. ❑ Moderate.
Bustling bistro with local dishes flavoured with herbs of Provence.

AU CHAPON FIN 3 rue Château-Fadaise, near Église St. Paul.
❑ 1200-1400, 2000-2200 Wed.-Mon. ❑ Moderate.
Classic French cuisine; for dessert try croquant villaret.

LES PERSIENNES 5 Pl. de l'Oratoire.
❑ 1200-1400, 2000-2200 Tue.-Sat. Closed Aug. ❑ Moderate.
Unlimited hors d'oeuvre bar and tasty, spicy local dishes.

L'OEUF À LA CÔTE 29 rue de la Madeleine, in the Old Town.
❑ 1200-2400. ❑ Inexpensive.
Open all day, including a salon de thé *serving refreshments between lunch and dinner. Try the prix fixe menu.*

LES HIRONDELLES 13 rue Bigot, near rue Porte de France, west of the Old Town.
❑ 1200-1500 Mon.-Sat. ❑ Inexpensive.
Lunch only but there is an excellent 50F menu, with wine included in the price.

LES CENTURONS 5 rue Porte de France, west of the Old Town.
❑ 1130-1400 Mon.-Sat. ❑ Inexpensive.
Hearty, noisy clientele; try the good-value 45F menu.

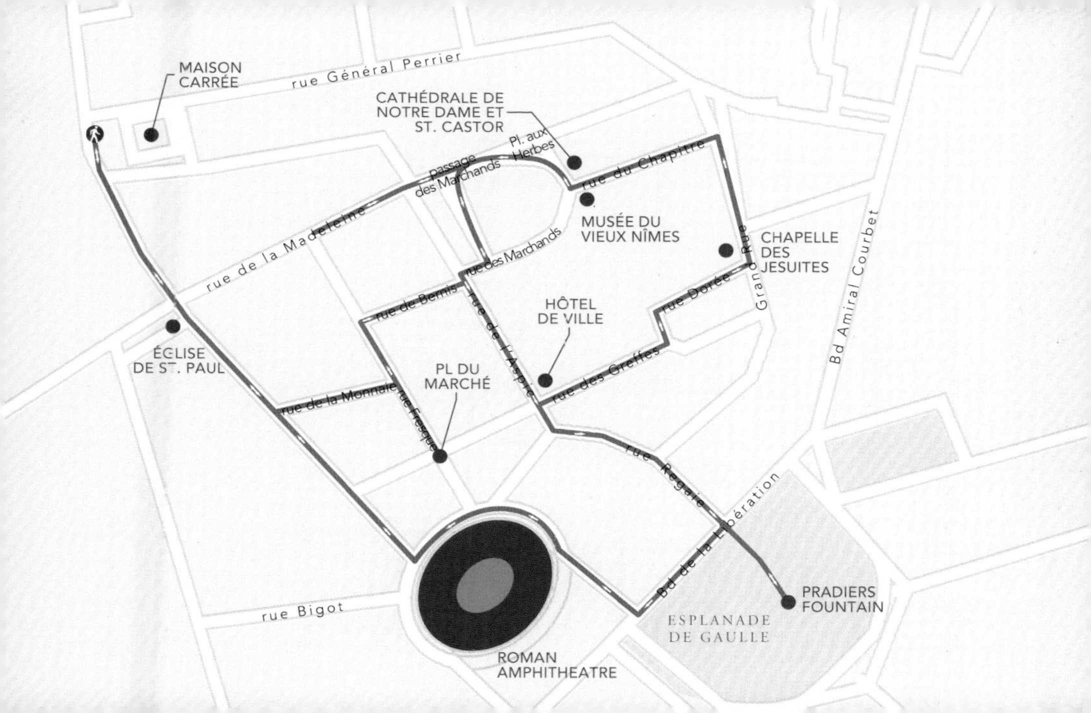
MAISON CARRÉE
rue Général Perrier
CATHÉDRALE DE NOTRE DAME ET ST. CASTOR
Pl. aux Herbes
passage des Marchands
rue du Chapitre
MUSÉE DU VIEUX NÎMES
rue de la Madeleine
rue des Marchands
CHAPELLE DES JESUITES
Grand Rue
Bd Amiral Courbet
rue Dorée
rue de Bernis
HÔTEL DE VILLE
rue de l'Aspic
ÉGLISE DE ST. PAUL
PL DU MARCHÉ
rue des Greffes
rue de la Monnaie
rue Fresque
rue Regale
Bd de la Libération
PRADIERS FOUNTAIN
rue Bigot
ESPLANADE DE GAULLE
ROMAN AMPHITHEATRE

Walk

1 hr 30 min-2 hr.
Start at the Tourist Office in a side street opposite Maison Carrée (see **NÎMES-WHAT TO SEE 1**). In Bd Victor Hugo visit the 19thC Romano-Byzantine Église de St. Paul with frescoes by Flandin inside. Opposite the Lycée Daudet take rue de la Monnaie to Pl. du Marché where the corn market was held in the Middle Ages. The fountains featuring a crocodile in chains (the Roman city arms commemorating Augustus' defeat of Antony on the River Nile), and palm tree are attractive. Turn left. In the rue Fresque are the 15thC Maison de l'Avocat des Pauvres at No. 16 and the 17thC Hôtel de Nors at No. 6. Turn right into rue de Bernis and note the 16thC Hôtel Meynier de Salinelles at No. 4. Turn right again into rue de l'Aspic with its smart shops, 17thC *hôtel* at No. 14 and carved porch walls with sarcophagi at No. 8. Turn left towards the 18thC Hôtel de Ville in rue des Greffes. Opposite is the 'Maison de Tartarin', formerly Hôpital Méjan, with its unusual clock. Walk through the 15thC vaulted alleyway with the Trésorerie Royale on your right. In the rue Dorée, where the medieval goldsmiths worked, are several *hôtels*, including L'Academie, at No. 16. Turn left into Grand Rue with the Chapelle des Jesuites and 18thC Hôtel Rivet which houses the École de Nîmes. Turn left into rue du Chapitre and look for the 17thC Hôtel de la Prévôté, and the 18thC Hôtel de Régis with its 16thC paved courtyard at No. 16. Opposite are the gardens of Ancien Evêché (Bishop's Palace) and the Musée du Vieux Nîmes, a 17thC episcopal palace (see **NÎMES-WHAT TO SEE 2**). In the Pl. aux Herbes is the Cathédrale de Notre Dame et St. Castor (see **NÎMES-WHAT TO SEE 2**) and at No. 9 rue St. Castor is the Renaissance presbytery. The Église de St. Eugénie and Francis I Hôtel are in rue de la Madeleine. Go through the passage des Marchands into rue des Marchands; No. 17 is a fine Renaissance building. Once again go into rue de l'Aspic: stop in Plan de l'Aspic and note the 'porte des Atlantes' at No. 2. Continue south past the rue de la Violette and the Roman Amphitheatre (see **NÎMES-WHAT TO SEE 1**) into the Esplanade de Gaulle gardens. The Palais de Justice is on one side, Pradier's fountain in the centre (see **NÎMES-WHAT TO SEE 2**), and Ave Feuchères, with its 19thC town *hôtels*, on the other. Walk back to the Tourist Office via the Bd Victor Hugo with the Église de St. Paul on the left.

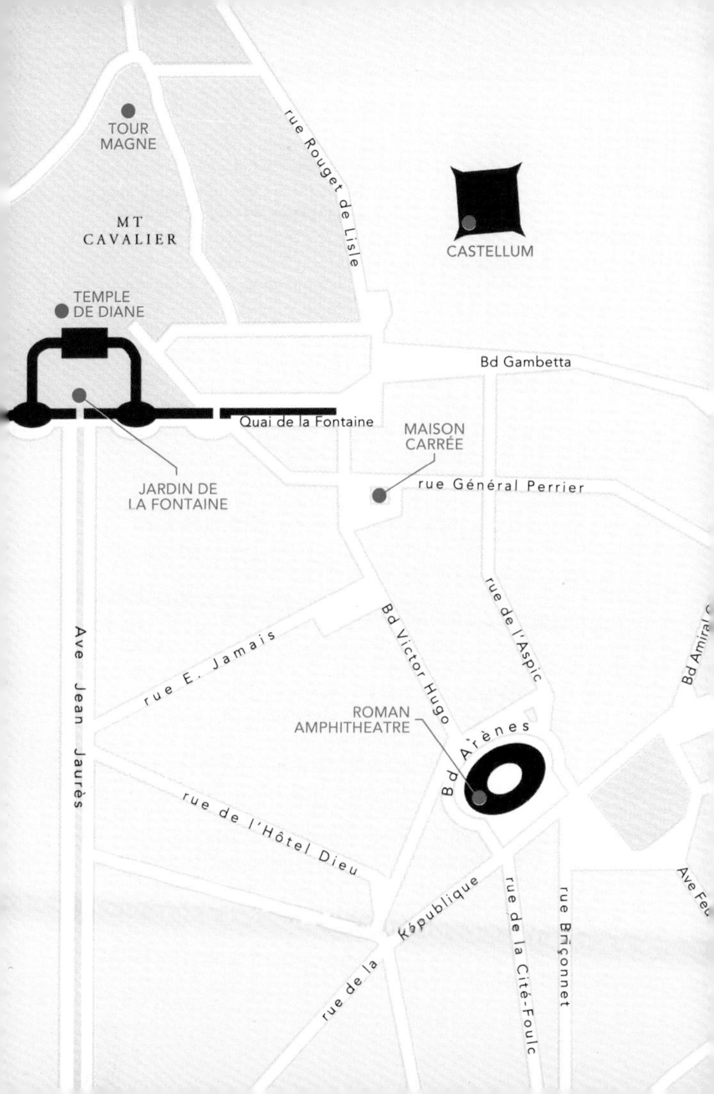

TOUR MAGNE

MT CAVALIER

rue Rouget de Lisle

CASTELLUM

TEMPLE DE DIANE

Bd Gambetta

Quai de la Fontaine

MAISON CARRÉE

rue Général Perrier

JARDIN DE LA FONTAINE

rue de l'Aspic

Bd Victor Hugo

Bd Amiral

rue E. Jamais

Ave Jean Jaurès

ROMAN AMPHITHEATRE

Bd Arènes

rue de l'Hôtel Dieu

Ave Feu

rue de la République

rue de la Cité-Foulc

rue Briçonnet

ROMAN AMPHITHEATRE Pl. des Arènes.
❑ 0800-2000. ❑ All-inclusive ticket for Roman monuments 30F.
The Roman architect Crispius Reburrus designed both the Nîmes and the Arles amphitheatres, but this is the best-preserved arena in the world (out of 70). It once held 21,000 spectators and measures 130 m by 100 m. See NÎMES-WALK, **Bullfights**, **Nîmes**.

MAISON CARRÉE rue Guizot, near the Tourist Office.
❑ 0900-1200, 1400-1700. ❑ All-inclusive ticket (see above).
Built in 1 BC by Emperor Augustus as the Capitol overlooking the Forum. Although rectangular in shape, 26.5 m by 13.5 m, it is known, oddly, as the Square House (Carrée). Inside are superb mosaics, statues of the Venus of Nîmes and of Apollo as an archer. See NÎMES-WALK, **Nîmes**.

TEMPLE DE DIANE On west side of the Jardin de la Fontaine.
❑ 0700-2300 July & Aug., 0800-2100 April-June & Sep., 0800-1900 Nov.-Mar. ❑ All-inclusive ticket (see above).
A ruined but romantic Roman temple discovered in 1745.

TOUR MAGNE On Mont Cavalier, at north end of the Jardin de la Fontaine.
❑ 0900-1900. Closed 1200-1400 out of season. ❑ All-inclusive ticket (see above).
Built in 15 BC, this octagonal tower was one of 19 in the town's defensive wall. There are 140 steps to the top but the reward is a superb view.

JARDIN DE LA FONTAINE 450 m west of Pl. Antonin.
❑ 0700-2300 July & Aug., 0800-2100 April-June & Sep., 0800-1900 Nov.-Mar. ❑ Free.
Gardens recreated in the 18thC under the slopes of Mont Cavalier. The setting for concerts and boules *contests. See* **Nîmes**.

CASTELLUM 200 m north of Bd Gambetta, 400 m east of the Jardin de la Fontaine.
Constructed in 19 BC, it was the distribution point for water brought from Uzès via the Pont du Gard into Nîmes. See NÎMES-EXCURSION.

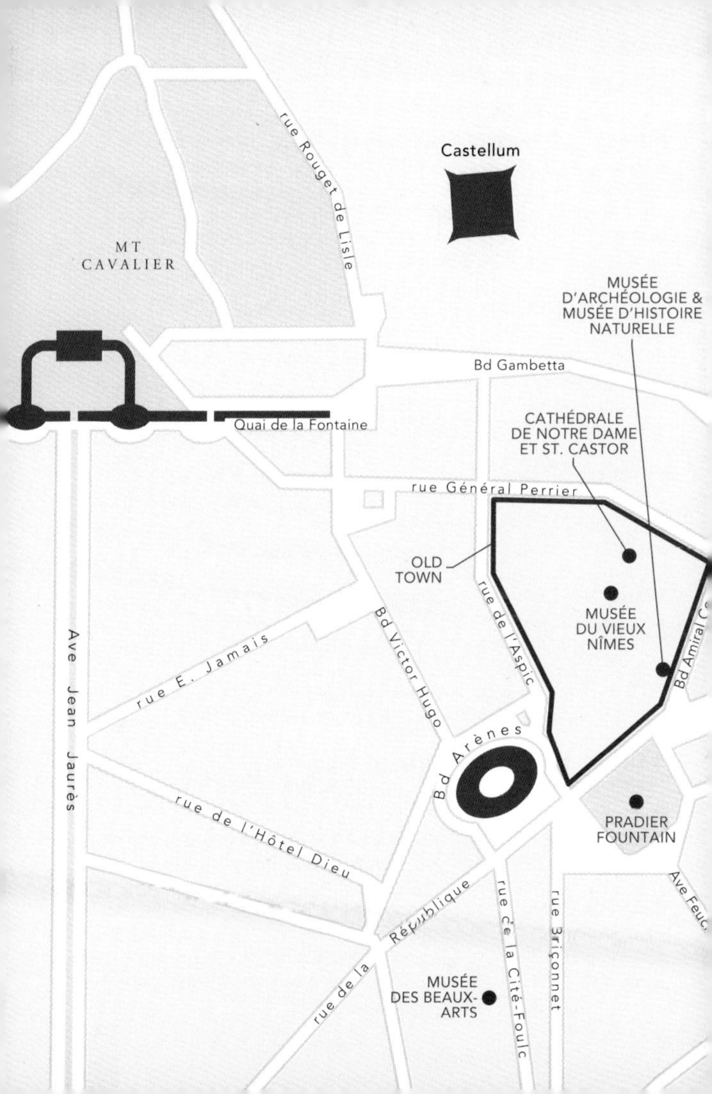
Castellum
MT CAVALIER
rue Rouget de Lisle
MUSÉE D'ARCHÉOLOGIE & MUSÉE D'HISTOIRE NATURELLE
Bd Gambetta
Quai de la Fontaine
CATHÉDRALE DE NOTRE DAME ET ST. CASTOR
rue Général Perrier
OLD TOWN
MUSÉE DU VIEUX NÎMES
rue de l'Aspic
Bd Victor Hugo
rue E. Jamais
Ave Jean Jaurès
Bd Arènes
PRADIER FOUNTAIN
rue de l'Hôtel Dieu
rue de la République
rue de la Cité-Foulc
rue Briçonnet
MUSÉE DES BEAUX-ARTS

CATHÉDRALE DE NOTRE DAME ET ST. CASTOR
Pl. aux Herbes in the Old Town.
❑ 0800-1800.
Partly 11thC in origin, the cathedral has a classical west facade with Old Testament scenes, and a Romanesque nave.

OLD TOWN
Streets of 17th and 18thC town mansions (hôtels) clustered around the cathedral. See NÎMES-WALK.

PRADIER FOUNTAIN 5-min walk east of the Amphitheatre.
An 18thC fountain set in large public gardens. See NÎMES-WALK.

MUSÉE DES BEAUX-ARTS rue de la Cité-Foulc, 200 m south of the Amphitheatre.
❑ 0900-1200, 1400-1800. Closed Tue. out of season. ❑ All-inclusive ticket to four museums 18F.
A major collection of paintings from the 16th-19thC French and European schools.

MUSÉE DU VIEUX NÎMES Pl. aux Herbes, next door to the Cathedral.
❑ 0900-1200, 1400-1800. Closed Tue. out of season. ❑ All-inclusive ticket (see above).
Housed in the old Bishop's Palace, it has two rooms devoted to bull-fighting history and techniques, plus medieval furniture, costumes, paintings and pottery. See NÎMES-WALK, **Bullfights**.

MUSÉE D'ARCHÉOLOGIE & MUSÉE D'HISTOIRE NATURELLE
13 Bd Amiral Courbet, off Grand Rue, on east side of Old Town.
❑ 0900-1200, 1400-1800. Closed Tue. out of season. ❑ All-inclusive ticket (see above).
The museums house Greek pottery of the 8thC BC, coins, statuary, and displays showing the life style of early Gallo-Roman families, as well as exhibits of local fauna and flora.

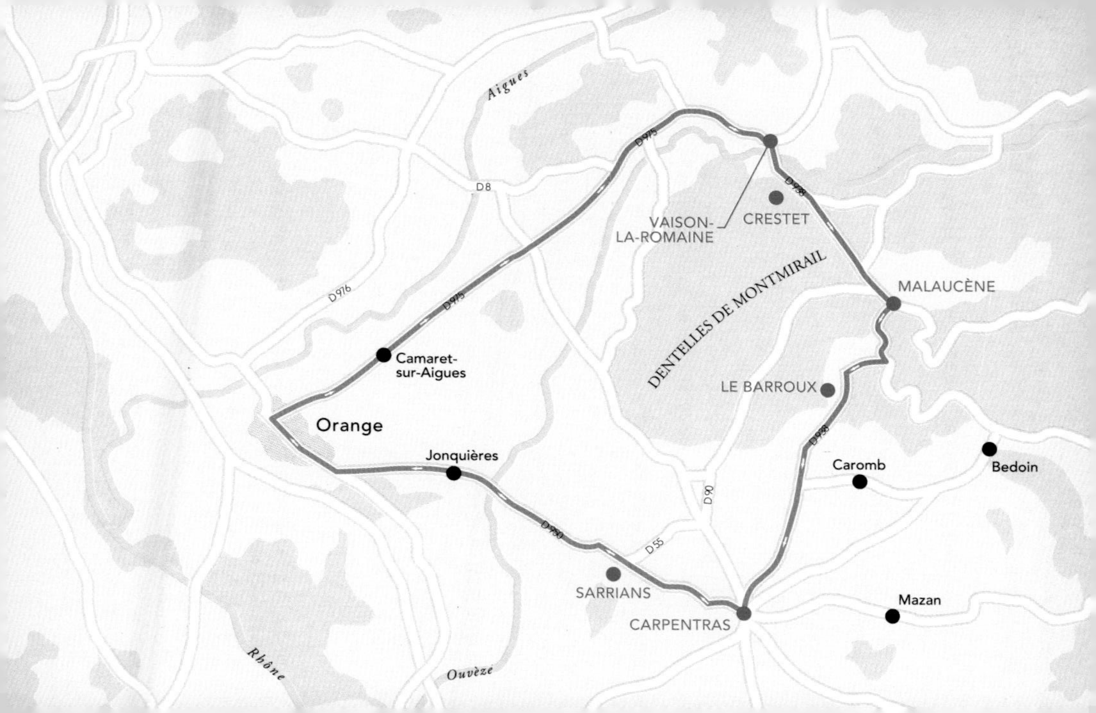
Aigues
D975
D8
VAISON-
LA-ROMAINE
CRESTET
D938
D976
DENTELLES DE MONTMIRAIL
MALAUCÈNE
Camaret-
sur-Aigues
LE BARROUX
Orange
Jonquières
Caromb
Bedoin
D90
D980
D55
SARRIANS
CARPENTRAS
Mazan
Rhône
Ouvèze

Excursion 1

A one-day excursion to Vaison-la-Romaine and Carpentras.

Leave Orange by the D 975 and head northeast via the village of Camaret-sur-Aigues, passing a small airport on the right, and following the course of the River Ouvèze.

27 km – **Vaison-la-Romaine** (pop: 5000). This town has two distinct characters. The medieval town (Haute Ville) with its 12thC castle stronghold stands proudly on a rocky spur on the south side of the river. Rights to hold Tuesday morning markets were granted to the citizens in 1483 by Pope Sixtus II. On the north side of the river, crossed by two bridges, one the Pont Romain, are the 5 ha excavated sites of the wealthy Roman town built in 12 BC comprising three areas – the Puymin Quarter, the Villasse Quarter and the Roman Theatre – with several temples, a marketplace, water cistern and basilica. It is one of the classic Roman sites in Europe and very popular, so try to visit out of season (guided tours 0900-1900; all-inclusive ticket for the three areas 18F). Other sights are the medieval Notre Dame de Nazareth cathedral and cloister, and the chapel of St. Quentin. Allow two hours for the Roman tour, another hour for exploring the Haute Ville and another hour for the cathedral and archaeological museum. From mid-July to early August a summer festival of ballet, opera, drama and classical music is held in the Roman theatre. Every third year (next in Aug. 1992) the international choral group festival, the Choralies, is staged. The Restaurant L'Escargot d'Or near Pont Neuf is moderately priced.

Drive 10 km south on the D 938 taking a short detour to the right on the D 76 to see the 12thC castle of Crestet, with the hills and olive groves of the Dentelles de Montmirail. Continue into Malaucène which

LA POSTE

has a 14thC Romanesque church built by Pope Clement V, a 15thC clock tower, the remains of a chateau and an 18thC hospital. The local honey, wine, cherries and cheese are excellent. The cool fountains, old plane trees and restaurant L'Eau Salée (closed in winter) with moderately priced Provençal cuisine, make this village worth a halt.
Drive south for 18 km on the D 938 via Le Barroux, with its restored Renaissance chateau on a hill on the right (1000-1900 July & Aug.; 10F). On the left are three villages in the foothills of Mt Ventoux: Bedoin, Caromb and Mazan.
55 km – Carpentras (pop: 27,000), where the poet Petrarch (see **A-Z**) spent his youth. This is a large market town, famous for fruit, vegetables and truffles (see **River Rhône**). The Cathédrale de St. Siffrein dates from 1404 and has Provençal paintings, the Jewish door and treasury. The large Hôtel-Dieu (charitable hospital), built in 1750, with hospital pharmacy, chapel and library (Mon.-Fri. times vary; 8F) is in a park in the south of the town. Opposite the Hôtel de Ville is the Jewish Synagogue. Built in 1367, it is the oldest in France and has a piscina, baking oven and rich-panelled sanctuary (1000-1200, 1500-1700 Mon.-Fri.; 10F) (see **Synagogues**). The only Roman legacy is the 1stC AD Arc de Triomphe erected by Emperor Augustus to commemorate victory over the barbarians. It is situated near the Palais de Justice and cathedral. The Inguimbertine library on Bd Albin Durand and two museums – the Comtadin with a folklore collection and the Duplessis which displays paintings by the local artists Parrocel and Duplessis – are housed in the Hôtel Allemand (1745), which has over 250,000 valuable tomes (0930-1830 Mon.-Fri.; all-inclusive ticket to cathedral treasury and four museums 6F). The other two museums are the Sobirats in rue du College (faïence and furniture) and the Lapidaire, rue des Saintes-Marie, which has an archaeological collection. If you are feeling hungry after your day's sightseeing L'Orangerie, 26 rue Duplessis and Le Coq Hardi, 36 Pl. de la Marotte will offer you moderately-priced meals, and you can eat inexpensively at Le Marijo at 73 rue Raspail.
Drive northwest for 8 km to Sarrians which has a former Benedictine Abbey, then continue 7 km on to Jonquières then the final 10 km back to Orange.

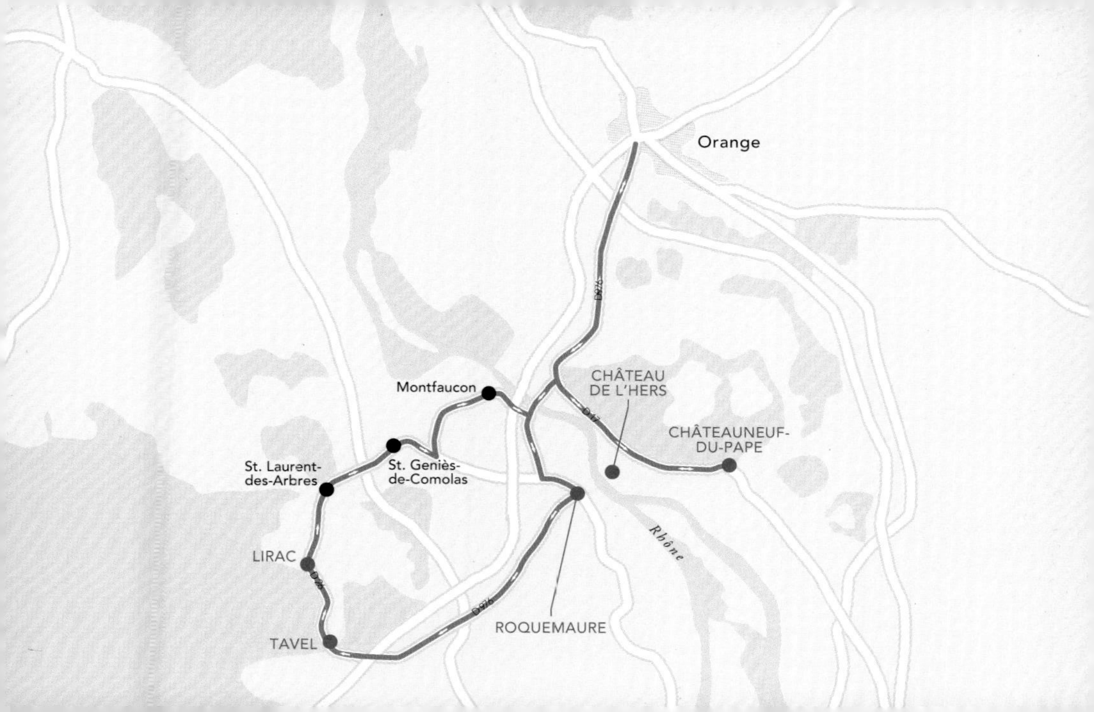
Orange
D976
CHÂTEAU DE L'HERS
D17
CHÂTEAUNEUF-DU-PAPE
Montfaucon
St. Geniès-de-Comolas
St. Laurent-des-Arbres
LIRAC
D26
TAVEL
D976
ROQUEMAURE
Rhône

Excursion 2

A half-day excursion southwest and west to the vineyards of Châteauneuf-du-Pape, Tavel and Lirac.

Drive southwest on the D 976, which runs parallel to the A 9, for 7 km and then join the D 17 for a further 6 km.

13 km – Châteauneuf-du-Pape. This is where the most famous red wine in Provence comes from. The ruined 14thC castle, built by the Avignon Popes, affords panoramic views over 3000 ha of vineyards. Thirty-five of the local wine growers offer tasting facilities. For a tasting session try the Association of Prestige & Tradition, rue de la République, then have lunch at Les Frères Jacques, rue Commandant Lemaître. After lunch you can go on to look at wine-making over the years at the Père Anselm Musée (0800-1200, 1330-1800). Another point of interest about the area is that Hannibal's elephants crossed the river near the Château de l'Hers, 2 km west of the village.

Retrace your steps along the D 17 and then go south on the D 976 crossing the Rhône.

23-km – Roquemaure (Gard department) has the 18thC Château de Cubières. Continue southwest on the D 976 for 8 km and turn right to get to the far side of the A 9.

33 km – Tavel. Fifteen growers including the local co-op offer tasting sessions which will allow you to sample France's most famous *vin rosé*. The hotel-restaurant Auberge de Tavel is good, but expensive, and has a wide range of local wines. Follow the D 26 north for another 5 km.

38 km – Lirac produces *rosé*, red and white wines. Taste them at the Château de Segries.

Return via the villages of St. Laurent-des-Arbres, St. Geniès-de-Comolas and Montfaucon (where Lirac wines have been grown since the 16thC). After Montfaucon take the D 976 to Orange.

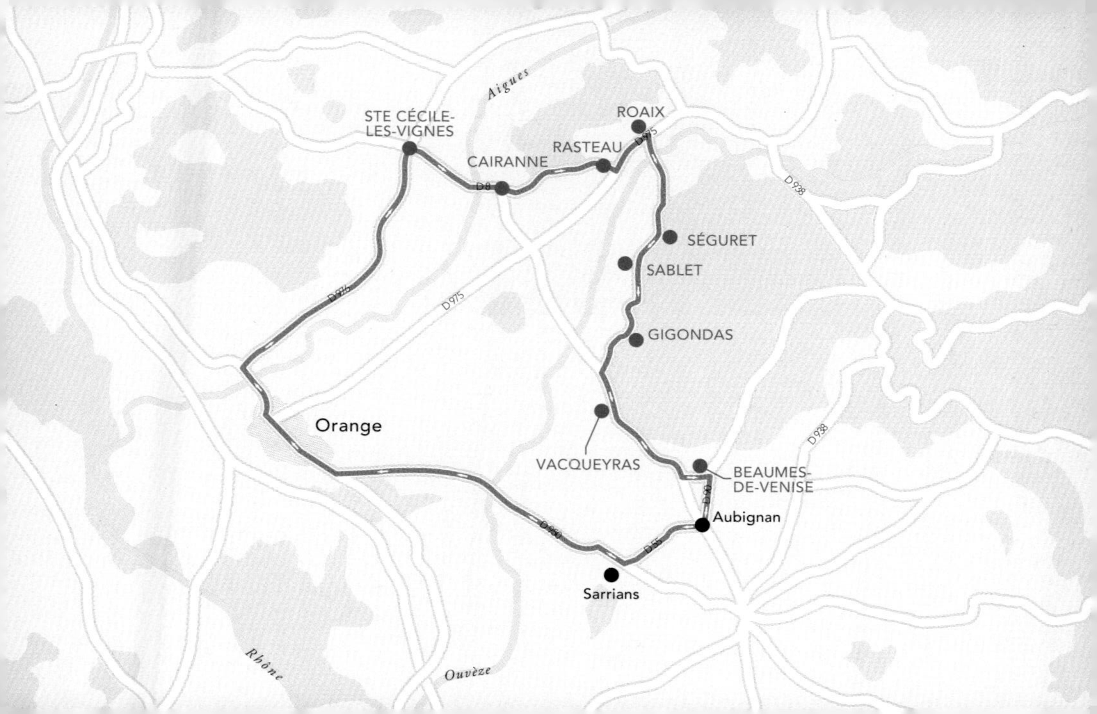
Aigues
STE CÉCILE-
LES-VIGNES
CAIRANNE
D8
RASTEAU
ROAIX
D975
D938
SÉGURET
SABLET
D976
D975
GIGONDAS
Orange
VACQUEYRAS
BEAUMES-
DE-VENISE
D938
D90
Aubignan
D950
D55
Sarrians
Rhône
Ouvèze

Excursion 3

A half-day excursion northeast and east to the wine regions of Rasteau, Gigondas and Beaumes-de-Venise.

Leave Orange by the N 7 heading due north for 3 km, passing the Roman Arc de Triomphe, and crossing over the River Aigues. Turn right and head northeast.

16 km – Ste-Cécile-les-Vignes. The town has the remains of the 14thC ramparts, a belfry and Côtes-du-Rhône vineyards.

Turn east on the D 8.

20.5 km – Cairanne. There is a 3rdC Gallo-Roman temple, a Templar tower and good views of the Côtes-du-Rhône vineyards. Take the minor road leading east out of the village.

30 km – Rasteau produces an unusual fortified tawny wine called 'Rancio'. Taste it at the wine co-op.

Drive north for 3 km on the D 975 to Roaix, a small wine village, which was once a Templar commanderie. Cross the River Ouvèze on the D 7 and follow the D 88 along the slopes of the Dentelles de Montmirail mountain range. After 4 km stop in Séguret, one of the prettiest villages in Provence (3 km further south is another at Sablet). Continue on the D 7 for a further 5 km.

42 km – Gigondas. The wine made here is preferred by many wine buffs to Châteauneuf-du-Pape. Fifteen growers offer tasting facilities – try the Cave des Vignerons in the small main square.

Drive due south on the D 7, join the D 8 and continue on to Vacqueyras. The wine co-op here is on the left-hand side of the road through the village and is called La Cave du Troubadour. 125 local farmers grow an excellent red wine, almost as good as neighbouring Gigondas. After your stop head southeast for 6 km.

51 km – Beaumes-de-Venise. The town is famous for its unique, perfumed, sweet white wine called *vin doux naturel.* This pale-golden fortified wine makes an excellent present. You can buy it from the local wine co-op.

Return via the D 90 to Aubignan, then head southwest on the D 55 for 5 km. At Sarrians take the D 950 northwest for 15 km to Orange.

ARC DE TRIOMPHE
Ave A. Artaud
Ave de l'Arc de Triomphe
rue du Nohle
Meyne
Ave Edouard Daladier
rue Lecour
rue Victor Hugo
Bd Aristide Briande
CATHÉDRALE
DE NOTRE DAME
DE NAZARETH
rue de la République
rue Contrescarpe
Meyne
PARC
GASPARIN
Pl. de
la République
rue St. Martin
rue St. Florent
MUSÉE
MUNICIPAL
Pl. des Frères
Mounet
THÉATRE
ANTIQUE
rue de Tourre
GYMNASIUM
CAPITOL
Ave Gen. Leclerc
PARC DE LA
COLLINE
ST. EUTROPE
rue St. Clément

THÉATRE ANTIQUE (Roman Theatre) Pl. des Frères-Mounet.
❑ 0930-1830. ❑ All-inclusive ticket for Roman monuments and Musée Municipal 18F.
A massive (103 m long and 36 m high) well-preserved theatre dating from the 1stC BC, which could hold 12,000 people. Note the reconstructed statue of Emperor Augustus above the central Royal doorway. Superb acoustics for the summer 'Chorégies' (opera productions).

GYMNASIUM Adjacent to the Théatre Antique.
❑ 0930-1830. ❑ All-inclusive ticket (see above).
Excavations have revealed buildings, dating from Emperor Augustus's time, which housed a large gymnasium, baths, changing rooms and running circuit (covering an area of 365 m by 80 m) and two temples.

CAPITOL Adjacent to the Gymnasium.
❑ 0930-1830. ❑ All-inclusive ticket (see above).
These remains of three temples dedicated to Jupiter, Juno and Minerva are built into the cliffs of St. Eutrope hill.

ARC DE TRIOMPHE On the N 7, 800 m north of the Théatre Antique.
The three-arched gateway was built in 36 BC to commemorate Roman military and naval victories. It is the third largest in existence.

MUSÉE MUNICIPAL (Musée Lapidaire) Opposite Théatre Antique.
❑ 0900-1200, 1400-1830. ❑ All-inclusive ticket (see above).
The museum houses interesting stonework finds from Roman sites, and a Roman land survey of the region engraved in marble in AD 77.

PARC GASPARIN cours Aristide Briande, near the Tourist Office.
Park with shady plane trees, cafés, restaurants and small hotels.

CATHÉDRALE DE NOTRE DAME DE NAZARETH
Pl. Notre Dame.
❑ 0800-1200, 1400-1900.
Provençal Romanesque-style building built over a temple to Diana.

Martigues

MT254849

Accidents & Breakdowns: Motorists involved in a traffic accident must complete a *constat à l'amiable* before the vehicle is moved. If the vehicle has been seriously damaged an expert's examination is advised prior to your return to the UK. The *constat à l'amiable* was introduced by the French insurance companies and it must be signed by the other party, but if a dispute arises and one of the parties involved should refuse to complete the *constat à l'amiable*, then the other party should immediately obtain a written report from a bailiff (*huissier*), which is known as a *constat d'huissier*. A bailiff can usually be found in any large town and charges a fee of 400F for preparing the report. Normally the police are only called out to accidents when persons are injured, a driver is under the influence of alcohol or the accident impedes the traffic flow.
If your vehicle breaks down obtain local assistance as there is no countrywide motoring club road service in France. For assistance on a motorway telephone the *brigade de gendarmerie* from an emergency telephone or service station. The police will contact a garage for you, but should it be necessary to remove the vehicle from the motorway for repair the choice of garage may be determined by the motorist. For AA members there is an emergency service, tel: 05302222 or 21872121. RAC members, tel: 21963530, and for motorists covered by a Europ Assistance policy, tel: 19-4416801234. The AA operates a port service in Calais, Boulogne and Cherbourg. See **Car Hire**, **Consulates**, **Driving**, **Emergency Numbers**.

Accommodation: Because of the popularity of the great arts festivals in midsummer in the main towns of Provence it is advisable to book hotels or camp sites in advance. There are five categories of hotel: * (basic), ** (comfortable), *** (very comfortable), **** (high class) and ***** (luxury). A double room costs anything between 150F and 1500F a night. The cheaper, more basic hotels are usually near the rail and bus stations. You will find booking facilities at the main Tourist Offices in each town. They offer help with last-minute difficulties, but will not necessarily get you the best deal. The Auberge de Jeunesse in each main town offers economic lodgings. See **Camping & Caravanning**, **Tourist Information**, **Youth Hostels**.

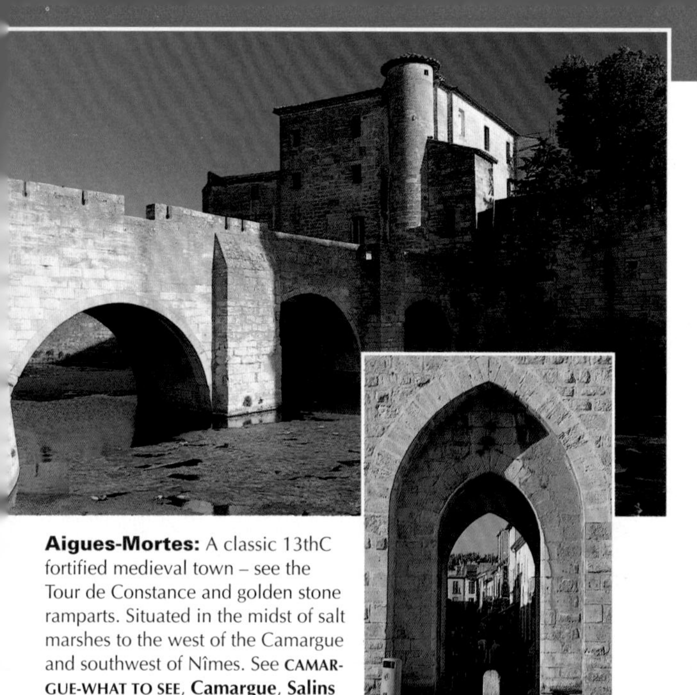

Aigues-Mortes: A classic 13thC fortified medieval town – see the Tour de Constance and golden stone ramparts. Situated in the midst of salt marshes to the west of the Camargue and southwest of Nîmes. See CAMARGUE-WHAT TO SEE, **Camargue**, **Salins du Midi**.

Airports: The main airport for Provence is Marseille-Marignane – 20 km west of Marseille, via the A 7, D 9 and D 20, tel: 42782100, 42899010 or 42890974. The air terminal is near Gare St. Charles and the Air France office is at Pl. de Gaulle, off La Canebière, tel: 91549292. For British Airways, tel: 91907710. Airport buses run from the terminal every 20 min and cost 36F.

Other airports in Provence are:

Nîmes-Garons	tel: 66700688.
Avignon-Caumont	tel: 90884349.
Aix-Les Milles	tel: 42210399.

Aix-en-Provence: Pop: 150,000. Aix-en-Provence has charm and a prosperous elegance unequalled in Provence, perhaps in all of France. It is twinned with the equally elegant European towns of Bath, Coimbra in Portugal, Perugia in Italy and Granada in Spain. It has been an important university town since 1413, and was a stop on the Grand Tour in the period 1700-1850. The town is small enough to explore on foot. In the old town look out for the fountains, the classic 17th-18thC town houses, the Cathédrale de St. Sauveur, and several fine museums. There are lots of enticing shops and a casino to tempt you in the evening. The cours Mirabeau, a wide, plane tree-lined cosmopolitan boulevard, is the best place to have an apéritif and watch the world go by. It was constructed in 1651 and its fountains, dignified town houses, and civilized shops and cafés make it almost unique in France (see **AIX-EN-PROVENCE-WHAT TO SEE**).
When the Romans founded Aquae Sextiae in 122 BC and made it the capital of Gallia Narbonensis, they little thought that, over 2000 years later, the famous hot (34°C) springs would still revive weary travellers in the spa Thermes Sextius. The town's heyday was during Good King René's reign in the 15thC. It was his home town and, as King of Naples, Duke of Anjou and King of Sicily, he employed the most talented musicians, poets and painters at his court (see **René of Anjou**). The exiled Scottish Jacobites made their court in Aix-en-Provence before moving on to Rome. However, it took an ugly, notorious firebrand to publicize the town. Count Gabriel Mirabeau (1749-91) was elected to represent Aix-en-Provence in 1789 during the French Revolution. His life was full of scandal, and he was once imprisoned for debt in the Château d'If prison (see **MARSEILLE-WHAT TO SEE**). Nevertheless, the most elegant street was renamed in his honour. Another famous citizen, better-known long after his death, was the Impressionist painter Paul Cézanne, whose paintings are so much in demand that the city has only eight modest examples, in the Musée Granet (see **AIX-EN-PROVENCE-MUSEUMS 1 & 2**, **Cézanne**).
The town boasts nine museums and three churches of note, and its 20thC claim to fame – apart from its intrinsic beauty and elegance – is the dazzling cultural festivals, which draw many thousands of visitors, it hosts each summer. Consequently hotels are always full in midsum-

La Rotonde

mer and early reservations are advisable. The town is classed as a *Ville d'Art* and the Tourist Office organizes town tours conducted by a guide who is a member of the Caisse Nationale des Monuments Historiques (1500-1700 Wed. with English-speaking guide; 45F). The main *hôtels*, Vieil Aix, the Quartier Mazarin and Bourg St. Sauveur can be seen on the tour. See AIX-EN-PROVENCE, **Events**, **Tourist Information**.

Albigensians: Albigensians were members of a 12thC religious sect which believed that the world was evil and created by the Devil. In Languedoc, particularly around Albi and Toulouse, and in parts of Provence, they gained many converts, until Pope Innocent III condemned them as heretics. A military crusade was launched against them under Simon de Montfort and the sect was brutally exterminated in 1208-09.

Arles: Pop: 51,000. The Greeks and Romans recognized Arelate (now modern Arles), the 'town in the marshes', as a key trading port and town due to its position on the banks of the Rhône, at the crossroads of the great Aurelian Way and the Agrippan Way. Hannibal's route from Spain to northern Italy took him through Arles, which then had a population double that of today. In 49 BC Julius Caesar founded a colony here for his sixth legion, a town with ramparts, tower and gates, and a water and sewerage system with public baths and lavatories of white marble. It was a trading centre for wine and olives, arms, gold and silver *objets d'art*, textiles and glass – and the home of the Roman imperial mint. Constantine the Great built a palace in Arles in AD 314, Emperor Honorius made the town the capital of the three Gauls – France, Spain and Britain – and later, in the 9thC, it was the

capital of the Kingdom of Arles, and then became a Crusader port. Arles has more Roman antiquities than any other town in Roman Provence. The oval-shaped Arènes, built in AD 1, once held 25,000 Romans who watched the black bulls from the Camargue fighting with gladiators. Three of its original towers still stand, as do most of the tiered stone seats, galleries and two rows of 60 arches. In the Middle Ages the citizens built a stronghold of 200 houses and a church inside the arena, and not even the ravages of religious wars nor the frenzy of the French revolutionaries has spoilt it. In 1825 the central houses were pulled down and the arena restored (see **ARLES-WHAT TO SEE 1**). The Roman theatre has been badly damaged over the centuries and it needs imagination to re-create what it looked like in Augustus' time. The stage wall, marble columns, some stone seating, curtain trench and orchestra pit remain, and much fallen statuary. It is enclosed in a walled garden and is used for summer concerts (see **ARLES-WHAT TO SEE 1**). The ruined Thermes Constantin are 4thC baths, part of Emperor Constantine's palace, and again it needs imagination to envisage them at the height of their glory (see **ARLES-WHAT TO SEE 2**).
The Place du Forum is a square in the centre of town with cafés, plane trees and a few original Roman columns. Note the statue of Frédéric Mistral who founded the Muséon Arlaten (see **ARLES-WHAT TO SEE 1**, **Mistral**). Ten minutes' walk southeast from the Tourist Office is the famous necropolis, the Alyscamps, adjacent to the canal de Craponne. Tombs and sarcophagi date from Roman times – some are in the Musée d'Art Chrétien (see **ARLES-WHAT TO SEE 2**).
Arles is a small town and the antiquities can be visited easily on foot. In addition to these there are four museums of considerable interest and three churches. Restaurants offer Provençal and Camarguais cuisine and are inexpensive. The town and region are also famous for the colourful paintings left to the world by Vincent Van Gogh (see **A-Z**).
See **ARLES**, **Events**, **Tourist Information**.

Authors: From Charles Dickens to Henry James, authors have visited Provence, fallen in love with the region and written glowingly of it. Gertrude Stein lived and wrote at St. Rémy-de-Provence and Lawrence Durrell lives near Nîmes, his novel *Monsieur* being set in Avignon.

Avignon: Pop: 100,000. Made famous by the nursery rhyme *Sur le pont d'Avignon*, by the fabulous 14thC architecture of the Palais des Papes, and more recently by the summer festival, this 14thC seat of the French popes is one of the best-loved cities in France. Ramparts encircle the town, and the River Rhône protects the west bank. Museums include the Calvet, Lapidary and Petit Palais, and the Cathédrale de Notre Dame-des-Doms houses two papal tombs. In the old quarter are *hôtels*, in the rue Roi-René and rue Dorée medieval guilds (*banastiers* = basket weavers, *teinturiers* = cloth dyers, *bonneterie* = hosiery, *carreterie* = stone masonry), and mendicant friars' chapels – black, white and grey (*noir, blanc, gris*). There is a wide selection of hotels and restaurants, but book early for the summer festival.
Avignon is an ideal centre for excursions by river and by train to the wine-growing areas in the north, to Cavaillon and the mountains and chateaux of the Lubéron to the east, and to the west to see the Pont-du-Gard. See **AVIGNON**, **Boat Trips**, **Events**, **Palais des Papes**, **Papacy at Avignon**, **Tourist Information**.

Banks: See **Currency**, **Money**, **Opening Times**.

Best Buys: Local craftsmen (*artisans*) are to be found in the villages of the Vaucluse selling their work. Other than crafts, look for Marseille

soap (made with olive oil), olives from Salon-de-Provence and Aix-en-Provence, herbs from St. Rémy-de-Provence, lime tea from Carpentras, truffles from Carpentras and Uzès, almond sweets from Aix-en-Provence, chocolates from Avignon and Tarascon, almond cakes from Nîmes and lavender from Aix-en-Provence. See **Food**, **Santons**, **Wines**.

Bicycle & Motorcycle Hire: Most SNCF stations, including Nîmes, Avignon and Arles will rent bicycles (to groups). In addition try the following:

Nîmes: Vespa, 6 Bd Alphonse Daudet, tel: 66676746.
Avignon: Dopieralski, 84 rue G. Puy, tel: 90863249.
Cycles Peugeot, Pl. Pie, tel: 90823219.
Arles: Dall'Oppio, 10 rue Portagnel.
Aix: Avis, 11 cours Gambetta, tel: 42216416.
Orange: Hertz, 11 Bd Daladier, tel: 90340034.
Les Saintes-Maries-de-la-Mer (for the Camargue):
Le Velociste, Pl. de l'Église, tel: 90978326.
Loca Sports, 30 Ave d'Arles.
Camargue Vélo, 37 rue Frédéric Mistral, tel: 90978209.

Prices vary between 55-70F per day, 300-400F per week. You will probably be asked for a deposit. Cycling is an excellent way of seeing the countryside in the Vaucluse and the Camargue. Scooters are not recommended, and neither are bicycles or scooters, in a city such as Marseille.

Boat Cruises: Loisirs Provence Mediterrannée operate across the Mediterranean to Corsica, north Africa and Sardinia; 36 rue St. Jacques, Marseille, tel: 91535747, and SNCM, 61 Bd des Dames, Marseille, tel: 91563200. GACM runs services to Château d'If, Ile de Frioul and the *calanques*, Quai des Belges, 1e, Marseille, tel: 91555009. Bâteau le Voltigeur operates out of La Ciotat; 11 Quai General de Gaulle, tel: 42831144. See **BEACHES**, **MARSEILLE-WHAT TO SEE**.
From the Quai L'Embarcadère at Avignon half-day excursions can be made along the River Rhône on the *Le Mireo* or *Le Provence* boats with meals and dancing aboard. Details are obtainable from Grands Bâteaux de Provence, allée de l'Oulle, tel: 90856225. There are also cruises up-

or down-river to Arles and Les Saintes-Maries-de-la-Mer. *Le Tiki III* sails from Les Saintes for 2-hr tours on the Petit Rhône, from the quay 2.5 km west of the town (Easter to October), tel: 90978168. See **River Rhône**.

Budget:

Hotel breakfast	25-50F
Lunch	50-250F
Plat du jour	30-50F
Museum/chateau ticket	10-30F
Bottle of *vin du patron*	25-35F
Hotel room for two	150-1500F
Picnic lunch for two from supermarket	70-90F

Bullfights: For 2000 years, since the Romans built their *arènes*, this has been a popular sport in the region. Nîmes is the home of France's major school, L'École Française de Tauromachie. *Courses Camarguaises* are in the local Provençal style, and involve the Camargue cowboys, *les gardiens*, called *rasetteurs* in the bullring, trying to snatch red roses (*cocardes*) from between the bull's horns. These fights are humane – nothing and nobody gets killed – but the more lethal Spanish fights *à la morte* are frequently on the agenda at Nîmes and Arles. See the Musée du Vieux Nîmes where two rooms are dedicated to the two styles of *tauromachie* – one entertaining, the other cruel and dangerous but exciting. Many small villages, for instance Barbentane, Châteaurenard and Fontvieille, organize local *courses Camarguaises*. See **ARLES-WHAT TO SEE 1**, **NÎMES-WHAT TO SEE 2**.

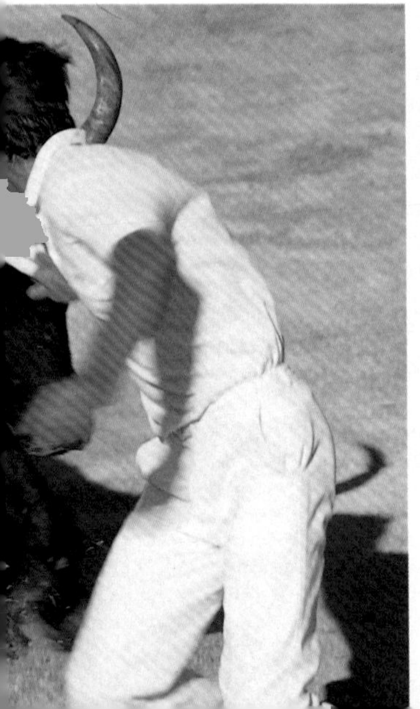

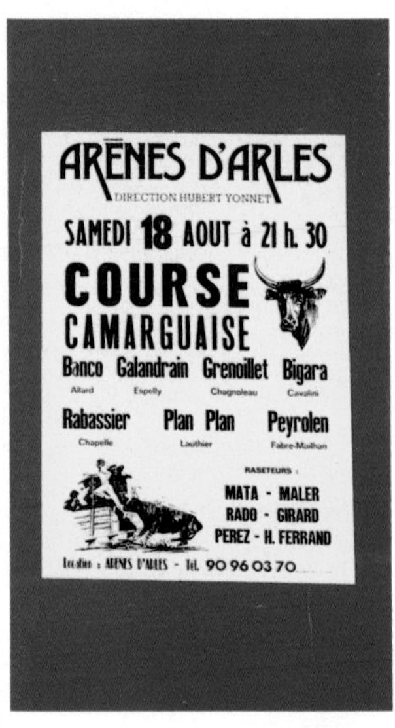

Buses: Bus stations (*gares routières*) and services are efficient and relatively cheap. The following are the main stations:

Marseille	Main station, Pl. Victor Hugo near SNCF. Enquiries 0800-1830, tel: 91081646. Services to Arles (Les Cars Verts de Provence); Avignon (Les Rapides du Sudest) and Cassis.
Nîmes	Bus station, rue Sainte Felicité, behind SNCF, tel: 66295400. City buses (TCN), tel: 66381540 – purchase a *carnet* of five tickets for 20F. Services to Avignon, Pont du Gard, Uzès and Pont St. Esprit (STDG); Aigues-Mortes and Le Grau du Roi (SNCF); St. Gilles and Les Saintes-Maries-de-la-Mer.
Avignon	Main station east of SNCF, Bd St. Roch, tel: 90820735. Town buses (TCRA) start at Tourelle de la République and Pl. Pie. Services to Vaison-la-Romaine and Orange (Cars Lieutaud); Châteauneuf-du-Pape and Orange (Rapides Sud-Est); Gard department, Alès and Pont du Gard (STDG); St. Rémy-de-Provence, Les Baux and Châteaurenard (Midi-Bus); Fontaine-de-Vaucluse (Cars Arnaud). No. 10 goes across the River Rhône to Villeneuve-lès-Avignon.
Arles	Buses leave from the SNCF terminal. Services to Les Baux, St. Rémy-de-Provence, Aix-en-Provence and Marseille (CVP); to Les Saintes-Maries-de-la-Mer and Nîmes (CCFC); to Aix-en-Provence and Marseille (Cars du Delta).
Aix	Bus station at rue Lapierre, near the Post Office, tel: 42260150. Services to Avignon, Arles and Marseille. CAP to Salon-de-Provence, Martigues-Lavéra and Marseille.
Orange	Bus station, cours Pourtoulles, near the Post Office tel: 90341559. Services to Avignon, Vaison-la-Romaine, Séguret and Carpentras. See **Tours**, **Transport**.

Camargue, La: La Camargue is southeast of Nîmes and southwest of Arles, about 80 km across at its coastal base with scores of small islands, lakes and the great Étang de Vaccarès in the centre. The area's population is less than 5000, of which 2000 live in the town of Les Saintes-Maries-de-la-Mer (see **A-Z**) – mostly gypsies and cowboy *gardiens* (complete with rodeo-style wide-brimmed hats) and their families. La Camargue has been a national park since 1970. 70% of the 800 sq

km region is marshland with an appropriate wildlife comprising storks, marsh harriers, black kites, buzzards, grey herons and cormorants. The skilled watcher may spot boar, beavers, badgers, weasels, foxes and, in

Gardiens

the lagoons, terrapins, water snakes and varieties of eel. Rice crops cover 4000 ha, and there are maize, a few vines producing *vin de table* and a constant desalination process gradually increasing the amount of cultivatable land. Trees are rare and ubiquitous clumps of bamboo act as windbreaks. Each year 600,000 tonnes of salt are produced from areas around Aigues-Mortes and Salin-de-Giraud (see **Salins du Midi**). The best time for a visit to La Camargue is spring or autumn, and be sure to take binoculars for bird-spotting, as well as anti-mosquito ointment. Renting a horse or bicycle is the best way to see the area. See CAMARGUE-WHAT TO SEE, **Bicycle & Motorcycle Hire**, **Events**.

Cameras & Photography: Films, video cassettes and flashes are widely available in all Provençal towns. Check with staff before using a camera in museums or art galleries, as there are usually restrictions.

La Camargue

Camping & Caravanning: Provence is an ideal place for a camping holiday. In the department of Bouches-du-Rhône there are 96 camp sites. Martigues-Lavéra is the most popular with 13 sites, La Ciotat has eight and Arles six. Altogether 49 towns and villages have sites. Information can be obtained from Comité Départemental de Tourisme des Bouches-du-Rhône, 6 rue du Jeune-Anarcharsis, Marseille, 6e, tel: 91549266. In the department of the Vaucluse there are 102 camp sites with no less than 76 towns and villages offering sites; Avignon for instance has five. Information from Chambre Départementale du Tourisme de Vaucluse, 2 rue St. Etienne La Balance, BP 147 Avignon 8, tel: 90864342. Nîmes, in the Gard department, has one site.
There are five categories of camp site, with four star being the most expensive, and *aire naturelle* the cheapest. Standards of comfort and opening/closing times vary considerably. For instance, at Avignon the four-star site of St. Bénézet charges 14F per person per night, children half price, plus an *emplacement* charge for a vehicle and caravan of 17F, or a vehicle and tent at 12F. Electricity connection costs an additional 13F. Camp sites are clean and well organized with a wide variety of additional services available including riding, tennis, swimming, bike rental, a play area for children or day nursery, laundry facilities, water points for caravans, and restaurants on or near the site.

Car Hire: To hire a car you must produce a passport and a current driving licence which has been valid for at least one year. A cash deposit is necessary, unless paying by credit card, and also proof of a local (hotel) address. The minimum age is 21-25, depending on the company. Be sure to check the basis of charge, i.e. a daily rate plus so much per km, or unlimited mileage. Third-party insurance is compulsory. Local agencies tend to be cheaper than the well-known international firms but check that they offer comprehensive insurance. Lower rates may be available out of season. Large towns have excellent facilities. Marseille has eight operators at Marignane airport and in town there are: Hertz, 16 Bd Charles-Nédélec; Avis, Gare St. Charles, Europcar, 7 Bd Maurice-Bourdet. In Nîmes there are seven operators at Nîmes-Garons airport plus, in town: Hertz, 39 Bd Gambetta; Avis, 1 bis rue de la République; Europcar, 17 rue de la République. In Avignon there is

Avis, 34 Bd St. Roch; Europcar, 27-29 Bd St. Roch. Aix has Thrifty Car Rental on rue Gustave Desplaces and in Carpentras Europcar is at 32 Bd Albin-Durand. Smaller towns have limited facilities so consult your hotel or local tourist office.

Cassis

Cassis: Pop: 6000. An attractive small resort 23 km east of Marseille, with beaches, a fishing port and casino, and vineyards on the slopes above the town. See **BEACHES, MARSEILLE-EXCURSION 1**.

Cézanne, Paul (1839-1906): The famous Impressionist painter who lived in Aix-en-Provence and found inspiration in the cypress and olive groves, the ochre-coloured villages and the forbidding grandeur of Mt Ventoux. See **AIX-EN-PROVENCE-EXCURSION 2, MUSEUMS 1 & 2**.

Chemists: There are plenty of chemists (*pharmacies*), identifiable by a green cross sign, in all towns in Provence. They are usually open 0900-1930 Mon.-Sat. and have a Sunday rota which your hotel manager or Tourist Office can tell you. See **Health**, **Opening Times**.

Climate: Provence's climate is excellent for most of the year, but beware of the strong cold north wind, the Mistral, which blows keenly down the Rhône valley. Average temperatures are 14-20°C in spring, 20-28°C in summer, 16-25°C in autumn and 11-14°C in winter. Spring and autumn are the best seasons for visiting, unless you are tempted by the summer festivals.

Complaints: It is very rare in Provence to be over-charged in hotels or restaurants, but nevertheless check every bill as you would at home.

Ensure that if you have chosen a fixed-price menu (there may be several), the waiter knows which one you have selected: 'Le menu à 110F svp'. If you have a serious complaint take it immediately to the manager of the establishment. If you get no satisfaction go to the Tourist Office and only as a final resort go to the police. See **Police**, **Tourist Information**.

Comtat Venaissin: The region east of Orange and Avignon owned by the Roman Holy See from 1274-1791, encompassing the towns of Cavaillon, Pernes, Venasque, Carpentras, Sault and Vaison-la-Romaine. See **AVIGNON-EXCURSION 1**, **ORANGE-EXCURSION 1**.

Consulates:

UK	24 Ave du Prado, Marseille, tel: 91534332.
USA & Canada	12 Bd Paul Peytral, Marseille, tel: 91549200.

Conversion Charts:

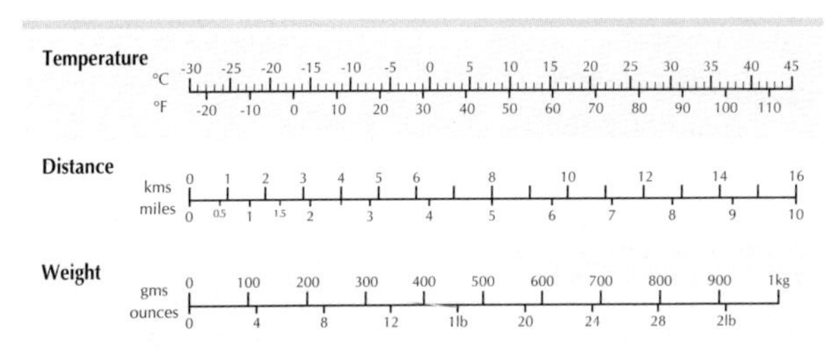

Credit Cards: See **Money**.

Crime & Theft: Special care should always be taken of handbags and wallets, etc. as pickpockets are rife in Marseille and, to a lesser extent, in Nîmes. Never leave your car unlocked and be sure to remove or hide any valuables. If you do have anything stolen, report the theft immediately to the nearest police station (*commissariat de police*) and

obtain an *attestation de vol* document so that you can claim insurance. You must inform your consulate at once if your passport is stolen. In emergencies, tel: 17; you will be put through to the local police station. See **Consulates**, **Emergency Numbers**, **Insurance**, **Police**.

Currency: The French unit of currency is the franc, which divides into 100 centimes. Bank notes are issued for 500F, 200F, 100F, 50F and 20F. Coins are 10F (two types, the older version is bronze-coloured, the newer ones are smaller with a brass rim and silver centre), 5F, 2F, 1F, 50c (all silver), 20c, 10c and 5c (all brass). See **Money**.

Customs Allowances:

Duty Paid Into:	Cigarettes *or*	Cigars *or*	Tobacco	Spirits *or*	Wine
EC	300	75	400g	1.5 *l*	5 *l*
UK	300	75	400g	1.5 *l*	5 *l*

Daudet, Alphonse (1840-97): The Provençal author of *Lettres de mon Moulin* and *Tartarin de Tarascon*. See his windmill near Fontvieille and a museum dedicated to him in Auriolles on the River Ardèche northwest of Pont St. Esprit. See **ARLES-EXCURSION**.

Dentists: See **Health**.

Disabled Travellers: For information about accommodation, transport, facilities and aids for the disabled, see the booklets *Touristes Quand Même* and *Guide des transports à l'usage des personnes à mobilité réduite* supplied by the Tourist Office. All TGV high-speed

trains can accommodate wheelchairs, and guide dogs are transported free. Other trains have a special compartment and an escalator for boarding. In Marseille contact Service de transport pour personnes handicapées physique, 18 rue d'Orient, 10e, tel: 91782167. See **Health**, **Insurance**, **Tourist Information**.

Doctors: See **Emergency Numbers**, **Health**.

Drinks: In France there are no licensing laws, so you can buy alcohol in bars and cafés at any time. House wines are sold by the litre (*une carafe*), half litre (*un demi-litre*) or quarter litre (*un quart*): a jug (*un pichet*) can hold either a quarter or half litre. Beer is usually lager. At meals plain water (*une carafe d'eau*) comes free. Coffee: ask for *un café* if you want a small strong black espresso, *un café au lait* for coffee with milk, and *un grand crème* for a large white coffee. Tea is available at *salons de thé*, and hot chocolate is popular, ask for *un chocolat*. Drinks are less expensive served standing in a bar or café (*au comptoir*). A pavement table may cost a great deal more. Try Provençal specialities such as *anis* or *pastis*, aniseed-flavoured apéritifs, and local wines such as Cassis, Rasteau, Beaumes-de-Venise, Gigondas and Châteauneuf-du-Pape. See **Wines**.

Driving: Apart from the rush-hour traffic in Marseille and Nîmes, driving in Provence is usually a pleasure, particularly out of season. You will need a valid national or international licence plus comprehensive insurance documents (preferably a Green Card), a nationality sticker, yellow filters for headlamps and a red warning triangle. The French drive on the right-hand side of the road, and at T-junctions, intersections and roundabouts the traffic from the right has priority.
The wearing of seat belts is compulsory for passengers in the front and recommended for those in the back. Try to make any long car journeys on a Sunday when trucks are forbidden by law to use the roads. There are emergency telephones approximately every 20 km on main roads and these are connected direct to the local police stations which operate 24 hours a day.
The speed limit in built up areas is 60 kph; on main roads 90-110 kph;

on motorways (*autoroutes*) 130 kph. Speeding offences carry a large fine from motorway police – the fine is payable immediately. French drivers are very competitive and a foreign numberplate is a challenge; resist the temptation to accept the challenge! Parking in the city centres of Marseille, Nîmes and Aix-en-Provence is always difficult, but less so in Avignon, Arles and Orange. Parking meters operate 0900-1900 but police or traffic wardens can impose fines or tow away vehicles parked illegally. If impounded telephone the town hall (*mairie*) to reclaim your vehicle. See **Accidents & Breakdowns**, **Car Hire**, **Petrol**.

Drugs: In France it is illegal to use or possess any form of narcotic and anyone caught trying to smuggle drugs into the country faces almost certain imprisonment.

Eating Out: Provençal cuisine is internationally famous and restaurants cater for every taste. By law all restaurants must display their prices outside and offer at least one fixed-price menu (*menu fixe, rapide menu, menu touristique*) as well as the usual 'à la carte' menu. These fixed-price menus, consisting of a choice between two or three dishes and courses, can cost as little as 50F, whereas the 'à la carte'

menu is always more expensive. The *plat du jour* is usually good, so ask the waiter what it is. In Marseille you will find good seafood restaurants and others serving dishes such as *couscous*. Restaurants traditionally serve lunch from midday until around 1400, and the evening meal from 1930-2100. Brasseries, bistros and *le drugstore* will serve a *plat du jour* at almost any time. Cafés serve a variety of drinks all day, as well as snacks, sandwiches and *croque-monsieur* (a toasted ham and cheese sandwich). Every Tourist Office will have a list of local restaurants, with addresses, telephone numbers, style of cuisine and some indication of price. In this guide an inexpensive meal would cost 50-100F, a moderate meal 100-200F and an expensive meal over 200F. See **RESTAURANTS-AIX-EN-PROVENCE, ARLES, AVIGNON, MARSEILLE, NÎMES, Drinks, Food, Tipping**.

Electricity: The voltage in France is 220V and a two-pin adaptor is required, available from most electrical shops, since plugs and sockets differ from those in Britain.

Emergency Numbers:

Police	17
Fire brigade (*sapeurs pompiers*)	18
SAMU (24-hr ambulance):	
Marseille	91499191
Nîmes	66670000
Emergency doctor (*SOS Médecin*):	
Avignon	90826500

For ambulances use the number given in the telephone box or, if no number is given, call the police (*brigade de gendarmerie*). In larger towns emergency help is available from the *police secours* (Emergency Assistance Department).

Entremont: Situated 3 km north of Aix-en-Provence on the D 14 are the excavations showing the foundations of this 2200-year-old fortified village (0900-1200, 1400-1800 Wed.-Mon.). Ramparts, towers, villas and gateways can be seen, and finds from the site are displayed in the Musée Granet. See **AIX-EN-PROVENCE-EXCURSION 1, MUSEUMS 1**.

Étang de Berre: An inland lagoon covering an area of 15,500 ha. It lies to the east of the Camargue and is bordered by the towns of Istres (west), Martigues-Lavéra (south) (see **MARSEILLE-EXCURSION 2**) and St. Chamas (north), and Marseille-Marignane airport (east). It is now a major oil-refining area.

Events: *January:* Carpentras, truffle markets, Fri. am in Pl. Aristide Briand; Cassis, Provençal nativity events.
February: Avignon, Cheval Passion (horse events), Palais des Expositions; *1st Tue. after 15:* Vaison-la-Romaine, Fair St. Quenin.
March: 26-27: Orange, Carnival.
April: Arles, Fête des Gardiens, with *corridas*; Les Saintes-Maries-de-la-Mer, bull-running *à la cocarde*; Villeneuve-lès-Avignon, Feast of St. Mark.
May: Arles, Fête des Gardiens, with *corridas*; St. Rémy-de-Provence, Fête de la Transhumance, with sheep and goats being driven through the streets to summer pastures; Salon-de-Provence, Fête des Bressons

Blazets; Nîmes, Whitsun Festival, with folklore events, bullfights and concerts; *24-25:* Les Saintes-Maries-de-la-Mer, gypsy pilgrimage; *27-30:* Orange, Spring Fair.
June: Marseille, Festival du Quartier, folklore concerts and dances; *1st week:* Cassis, Fête de la Mer; *mid-month:* Les Saintes-Maries-de-la-Mer, Grande Fête Votive.
July: Villeneuve-lès-Avignon, Summer Arts Festival in the Chartreuse; *1st two weeks:* Vaison-la-Romaine, International Folklore Festival; *1st Sat.:* Martigues-Lavéra, Venetian-style fête on the canals; *9:* La Ciotat, Venetian-style harbour fête, with jousting and fireworks; *14:* Bastille Day, celebrated with pageants, processions, parades, etc.; Fontvieille, Provençal dances at Daudet's mill; *last three weeks:* Avignon, International Drama Festival in Palais des Papes; Nîmes, International Folklore Festival; *end of month:* Beaucaire, annual fête to commemorate famous medieval trade fairs.
August: beginning of month: Marseille, Fête St. Pierre, with jousts at L'Estaque harbour; *1st weekend:* Châteauneuf-du-Pape, medieval *artisanal* fair; *14-17:* Les Saintes-Maries-de-la-Mer, Feria Saintoise, with *courses, corridas* and fireworks; *15:* Gordes, festival and *spectacle equestre*; *3rd week:* Séguret, Provençal festival.
September: Aix-en-Provence, Gathering of Félibres societies to celebrate Mistral anniversary; Arles, Fêtes de Premines du Riz; Camargue festival for ten days; *beginning of month:* Cassis, Fête des Vins de Cassis; *4th Sun.:* St. Rémy-de-Provence, *fête votive, courses,* dances and concerts.
October: Sun. nearest 22: Les Saintes-Maries-de-la-Mer, Fête of St. Marie with procession to and blessing of the sea.
November: Avignon, baptism of Côtes du Rhône Primeur wines after vintaging.
December: International Santons Fair at Marseille, Arles, Tarascon and Apt; *24:* Midnight Masses at Les Baux-de-Provence, Séguret, Fontvieille and Allauch. See **Music, Music Festivals**.

Félibrige: A Provençal society founded near Avignon in 1854 by Frédéric Mistral, the poet (see **A-Z**), Roumanille, a schoolmaster, Aubanel, the printer, and others. The society's aim was to preserve the

folklore traditions of Provence in literature, art, dress, furniture, customs and language. When Mistral won the Nobel Prize for literature in 1905 he established the Muséon Arlaten, a folklore museum, in Arles. The Musée Théodore Aubanel (dedicated to another of the society's founders) is in Avignon, and both will interest visitors to the region. See **ARLES-WHAT TO SEE 1, AVIGNON-WHAT TO SEE.**

Fontaine-de-Vaucluse: A million visitors come each year to see the source of the Sorgue river emerging from a huge rock face 5 km west of Gordes. This natural wonder is also noted for the Italian poet Petrarch (see **A-Z**) who lived here between 1337 and 1353 and composed 366 sonnets to his 'Laura'. See **AVIGNON-EXCURSION 1.**

Food: Provençal cuisine is tastier and more colourful than that in any other region in France. Local herbs include basil, fennel, thyme, tarragon, rosemary, saffron, bay leaves and sage. Garlic (*ail*) is used to flavour the majority of dishes and the 'black diamond' or truffle is used

to enhance omelettes. Tomatoes, artichokes, red and green peppers, asparagus, courgettes and aubergines are the main vegetables. Olive oil is used frequently in *cuisine Provençale.*

Hors d'oeuvres might be anchovies, tuna and fresh sardines or *tapenade,* a colourful paste of anchovies, olives, capers and tuna mixed and pounded. *Ratatouille* is a popular vegetable dish consisting of courgettes, tomatoes, aubergines, green peppers and garlic blended with lots of olive oil. *Pistou* is a vegetable soup full of flavour and colour with grated cheese on top.

Fish dishes: *Bouillabaisse* is made from as many as 30 to 40 ingredients: specifically *rascasse* (scorpion fish), *congre* (conger eel), *grondin* (gurnet) and John Dory, bass, sea perch, mussels and prawns, with perhaps a bright red lobster on top. The seasoning is an art in itself with all the herbs mentioned above plus a dash of brandy or white wine. *Bourride* is based on white fish such as *dourade,* turbot and monkfish

with *aioli* sauce (garlic mayonnaise). *Rouille* is a sauce of red pepper and garlic, and *brandade de morue* is a purée of salt cod, with olive oil, garlic and truffles. Other popular fish dishes are *moules marinières* (a mussel soup with garlic), *oursins* (sea urchins), *loup de mer* (sea bass), *rouget* (red mullet) and *clérisses* (clams). River fish dishes are popular too; trout, shad, crayfish (*écrevisses*) from the rivers Sorgue, Auzon or

Ouvèze, *carpe farcie* (stuffed carp) or *catigau* (Rhône smoked eel). Meat dishes include *lièvre du Ventoux* (hare), *agneau des Monts du Vaucluse* (mountain lamb), *civet de porcelet à l'Avignonnaise* (piglet stew), *la grillade des mariniers du Rhône* (traditional Rhône boatmen's grilled beef), as well as duck, rabbit and small birds (thrush, lark, quail or pigeon). In the hinterland of the Vaucluse expect to find *jambon cru de Malaucène, pâté de grives* (thrush pâté), *la caillette aux herbes* (quail in herbs) and *truffes sous la cendre* (Ventoux truffles). *Sanglier* (wild boar) is a great delicacy, often served as a pâté or terrine laced with local *marc* (brandy).
Goats' cheeses (eaten very young and fresh) will be on the menu, and among the sweets you will find *calissons* or *papalines d'Avignon, berlingot* sweets from Carpentras, nougat from Sault and almond cream gateaux called *caladons*. See **Best Buys**, **Eating Out**, **Markets**.

German Occupation: During World War II the Wehrmacht and SS used ferocious tactics to counter the widespread Resistance movement in the Provence area. In January 1943 they blew up a large area of the Vieux Port in Marseille and expelled 40,000 of its inhabitants overnight. Salon-de-Provence was a centre for the Resistance; Jean Moulin, the movement's leader, was brutally killed by the Gestapo in 1944. His tomb is in the Panthéon in Paris, and a memorial to him stands beside the N 7. The Chaîne des Côtes, near Lambesc, east of Salon-de-Provence, was another Resistance centre (see **AIX-EN-PROVENCE-EXCURSION 1**) and Gordes was another practically destroyed in 1944. During their retreat north in the summer of 1944 the Germans perpetrated much pointless last-minute damage, such as the burning of the chateau in Châteauneuf-du-Pape.

Health: Medical treatment is available to all citizens of EC countries through the French social security system. Residents of the UK should obtain a form E 111 from the DSS before departure. You will have to pay for any treatment you receive, then claim it back on your return to Britain. Even an ordinary visit to the doctor costs about 100F, so it certainly pays to take out medical insurance beforehand. Lists of doctors and dentists, including those available on Sundays and holidays, can

be obtained from police stations, chemists and probably from your hotel.

Hospitals:	Arles	90966410
	Aix-en-Provence	42239800
	Orange	90344633
	Vaison-la-Romaine	90360458

See **Disabled Travellers**, **Emergency Numbers**, **Insurance**.

Hospitals: See **Emergency Numbers**.

Insurance: You should take out comprehensive travel insurance covering you and your family, if travelling with you, against theft and loss of property, car and money, as well as medical expenses, for the duration of your holiday. Your travel agent, the AA or RAC will recommend a suitable policy. See **Crime & Theft**, **Driving**, **Health**.

Laundries: Hotels usually offer a laundry service. All towns in Provence now have self-service, coin-operated launderettes (*laundromats, laverie automatique*) usually open 0800-1900.

Le Corbusier (1887-1965): The working name of Charles Edouard Jeanneret, a highly controversial Swiss architect who built the huge concrete Cité Radieuse or Unité d'Habitation. 2000 people live and work in this 16-storey township on stilts, comprising 337 flats in 23 different styles. During the period 1946 52, while it was being built, the avant-garde architectural style of the structure caused a sensation. See **MARSEILLE-WHAT TO SEE**.

Legends & Myths: These abound in Provence. Many of them are associated with members of the Holy Family who are reputed to have landed at Les Saintes-Maries-de-la-Mer: the Virgin Mother's sister, Ste Marie Jacobe, and the mothers of the Apostles James and John, Ste Marie Salomé, and Ste Marie Magdaleine. Four other saints accompanied them; Marthe, Lazare, Maximin and the blind Suedonius, as well as black Sarah, their African servant, who was adopted by the nomads and gypsies as their patron saint. Marthe is famed for taming the Rhône monster – the Tarasque – at Tarascon (see ARLES-EXCURSION, AVIGNON-EXCURSION 2). According to legend Lazare, with his sisters and St. Maximin, lived for some time in a catacomb in the cemetery of the Abbaye Saint-Victor in Marseille (see MARSEILLE-CHURCHES). Ste Maximin and Suedonius then went to Aix-en-Provence where the former became its first bishop and was martyred for his faith. The tombs in the crypt of the Basilique de St. Maximin-la-Ste-Baume 40 km east of Aix-en-Provence are venerated as being those of Ste Marie Magdalene and St. Maximin. See AIX-EN-PROVENCE-EXCURSION 2.

Les Baux-de-Provence: The famous medieval hilltop-village, situated 19 km northeast of Arles and 10 km south of St. Rémy-de-Provence. It was once the home of the warrior Lords of Baux, in whose courts troubadours (see **A-Z**) sang their romantic ballads. See ARLES-EXCURSION.

Les Saintes-Maries-de-la-Mer Pop: 2000. This small town is noted for its gypsy pilgrimages and as the base for ornithological excursions into the Camargue. See BEACHES, CAMARGUE, **Camargue**, **Events**, **Legends & Myths**, **Pilgrimages**.

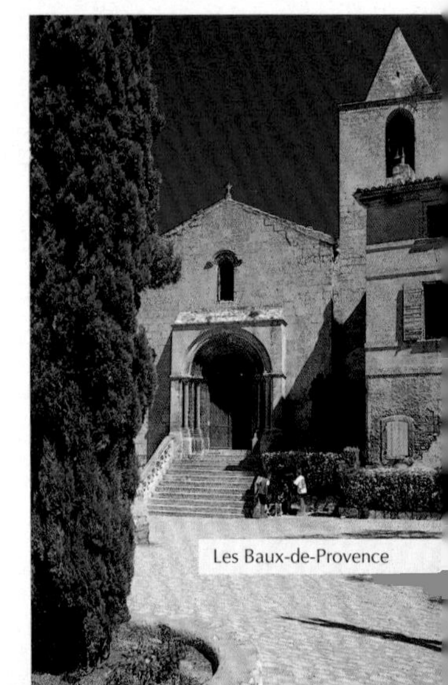
Les Baux-de-Provence

Lost Property: If you lose anything in one of the large towns you should contact the Bureau des Objets Trouvés in large towns. In Marseille it is at 2 rue du C.-Becker, 2e, tel: 91919040, and in Nîmes at 6 Pl. de l'Oratoire, tel: 66678429. In smaller towns ask the hotel or camp-site manager for advice or visit the police station.

Markets: The open-air markets in Provence have to be seen to be believed; colourful fruit, vegetables and flowers, and rather smelly fish markets. Every town and most villages have markets, usually in the morning only. Marseille, for instance, has 24 food and produce, two fish and six flower markets. Ask at the Tourist Office for times and places. Some unusual markets are the *marchés aux truffes* at Carpentras and Richerenches, and the *marchés d'artisans* (local crafts markets) at Avignon, Châteauneuf-du-Pape and L'Isle-sur-la Sorgue. See **Best Buys**, **Food**, **Shopping, Tourist Information**.

Marseille: Pop: 880,000. Marseille is the oldest city in France, founded in 600 BC by Greek traders from the Aegean. The village-port they named Massalia is now the second largest French city, and, with the Fos and Étang de Berre (see **A-Z**) complexes, is France's number one port. The capital of Provence, it is also known as the 'Gateway to the Orient', and you will see people of many different nationalities walking down the famous La Canebière towards the Vieux Port and the Quai des Belges. There, smart yachts and fishing boats float under the stern gaze of the golden Virgin on the summit of the Basilique de Notre Dame-de-la-Garde.

Marseille has the reputation of being a brash, modern, mildly dangerous city – although the local crime rate is less than that of Paris. Certainly at night take sensible precautions and keep to well-lit streets away from the North African quarter.
Few people realize how much Marseille has to offer the visitor. The Tourist Office will give you advice about hotels. There are 150, including 82 economic one-star hotels with double rooms priced at 100-150F, as well as four-star hotels such as Sofitel Vieux-Port and Grand Hôtel Noailles. Make sure you get a copy of *Nouvelles de Marseille*, an excellent monthly booklet which has a map showing the Métro stations, 11 museums, the opera and 17 theatres, as well as six sandy beaches and seven parks. Since all large cities have a parking problem try to find a hotel with private parking or put your car in a paying car park (cours Julien, cours d'Estienne d'Orves, Gare St. Charles and Gambetta). The Tourist Office has a city tour every day at 1000 from 4 La Canebière, which takes you to the famous but sleazy La Canebière, Porte d'Aix, the cathedral, Église de St. Laurent, Hôtel de Ville, Basilique de Notre Dame-de-la-Garde, Corniche President Kennedy, Parc Borély, the Le Corbusier housing development, and back to the Tourist Office. It costs 90F and is a good way to start your visit. See BEACHES, MARSEILLE, **Boat Cruises**, **Events**, **Métro**, **Tourist Information**.

Métro: The Marseille Métro (M) has two lines: the M1 (Castellane–La Rose) and the M2 (Bougainville–St. Pierre or Ste Marguerite). There are 22 stations and a *carnet* of six tickets for the Métro or bus costs 31F. The service is run by RTM, 7 rue Reine-Elizabeth, tel: 91919210, and you can get a free RTM plan – *Guide du Réseau* – from the Tourist Office.

Mistral, Frédéric (1830-1914): The leading Provençal folklore poet who won the Nobel prize for literature in 1905, headed the Félibrige (see **A-Z**) and founded the Muséon Arlaten in Arles. See ARLES-WHAT TO SEE 1.

Money: Every town in Provence has a wide choice of banks which open 0830-1630 Mon.-Fri. There are also exchange facilities at airports

and main-line railway stations (Marseille, Avignon, Nîmes), as well as in most Tourist Offices (useful at weekends). Most main post offices usually also have currency exchange facilities, often with a low rate of commission. The major cities have a number of bureaux de change in the centre and near the SNCF. Exchange rates and commission charges do vary, so it pays to look around.
Credit cards are widely accepted, with Visa (*Carte Bleu*) being the most common. Traveller's cheques are probably the safest way to carry holiday money and can be used in many locations, but not in the smaller hotels and restaurants. They are easy to change at any bank or bureau de change, don't forget to take your passport when you want to change some. See **Currency**.

Museums: Provence has a wide range of interesting museums covering a multitude of subjects: archaeology, folklore, military history, local flora and fauna, the Foreign Legion, tapestries, *santons* (see **A-Z**) and ceramics, as well as the more traditional beaux-arts. They are frequently closed on Tuesdays, and the smaller ones also close between 1200-1400. You should expect to pay an entrance fee ranging from 8-25F depending on the importance of the collection. See **MUSEUMS-AIX-EN-PROVENCE, MARSEILLE**.

Music: Provence has more great music festivals than any other part of France, in particular the International Music Festival in Aix-en-Provence. Aix also has the Big-Band Jazz Festival, Orange its Chorégies of opera and choral productions and Vaison-la-Romaine holds opera and classical music concerts in the Roman theatre. The Festival of Avignon has something for every music lover (12 official plus 35 fringe locations). The opera and theatres in Marseille have a constant flow of excellent musical events. Even smaller towns such as Apt have music festivals (Whitsun). Early booking is advisable in every case, either via the Tourist Office or at the major festivals' special offices: Avignon, Bureau du Festival, BP92, 84006 Avignon, tel: 90826708; Aix-en-Provence, Palais de l'Ancien Archevêché, tel: 42231120; Orange, Maison des Chorégies, Pl. Sylvain, tel: 90341552. See **Events, Music Festivals, Tourist Information**.

Music Festivals: Below is a list of the main music festivals, which largely take place in the summer.
June: Marseille, Festival du Quartier, folklore concerts and dances; *end of month:* St. Rémy-de-Provence, Musical Fête, with folk events; *end of month*: Sorgues, International Jazz Festival.
July: Aix-en-Provence, International Music Festival, classical, jazz, blues; Arles, International Festival of Drama, Dance and Music in Roman Theatre; Nîmes, International Jazz Festival; Orange, International Music Festival, operas and classical concerts in Roman Theatre; *14:* Fontvieille, Provençal dances at Daudet's mill; *mid-July to mid-August:* Vaison-la-Romaine, Les Choralies, international choral music events in Roman Theatre; *mid-July to mid-August:* Carpentras, Festival of Theatre, Ballet, Dance and Music; Nîmes, International Folklore Festival; *last three weeks of August:* Uzès, Festival of Classical and Modern Music.

Newspapers: A wide range of newspapers can be bought at pavement newsstands in Marseille, Nîmes, Avignon and Aix-en-Provence. However, English-language papers are rare. See **What's On**.

Nightlife: Marseille has the most sophisticated nightlife in Provence. Consult the monthly *Nouvelles de Marseille* which lists opera, ballet, a dozen theatres, four jazz clubs, six cabarets and five café-théatres. Nîmes has eight music halls, cabarets and discos. Consult the *Informations Pratiques* pamphlet and try an evening out at the café-theatre Le Titoit de Titus, 6 rue Titus. Aix-en-Provence has six theatres and seven nightclubs and discos, as well as the Municipal Casino, in the Pl. de la Rotonde, for those who like to gamble. Avignon has a wide range of entertainment advertised in its brochure *Avignon Pratique*, including theatres, jazz clubs and discos. The Grand Siècle is popular. See MARSEILLE-NIGHTLIFE, **Tourist Information**.

Nîmes: Pop: 130,000. The *préfecture* town of the Gard department, Nîmes is on the boundary of Provence, to the east, and Languedoc, to the west. Unusually, it was not established near a river, but on a spring which gushes out of the rock at the foot of Mont Cavalier. The spring is

now neatly channeled into the Jardin de la Fontaine (see **NÎMES-WHAT TO SEE 1**). The Celts called the spring Nemausus. When Emperor Octavius defeated Antony, he settled his Egyptian army veterans in the Colonia Augusta Nemausensis (their crest was a crocodile chained to a palm tree), in Nîmes. Many important roads converged on Nîmes (and still do) from Spain, Italy and northern France, including the Via Domitia, and thus the city prospered and became known as 'The Rome of France'. Two buildings have survived from that era: the beautiful, classical temple called La Maison Carrée, the oblong-shaped capitol facing the Roman forum; and Les Arènes, the great amphitheatre which is almost a replica of that at Arles (see **NÎMES-WHAT TO SEE 1**). Between 1229 and 1809 the amphitheatre

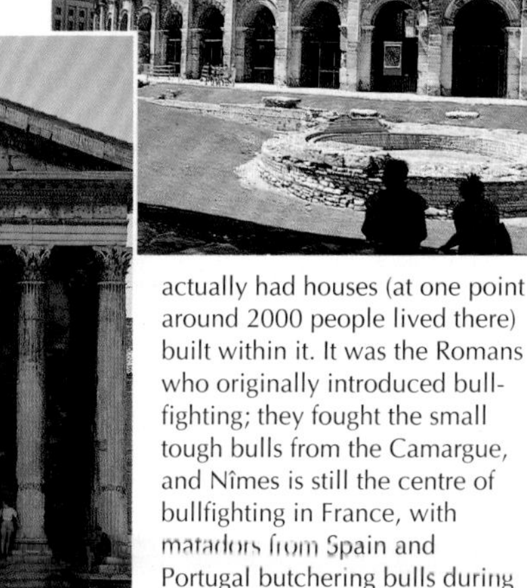

actually had houses (at one point around 2000 people lived there) built within it. It was the Romans who originally introduced bull-fighting; they fought the small tough bulls from the Camargue, and Nîmes is still the centre of bullfighting in France, with matadors from Spain and Portugal butchering bulls during the long, hot summer season – definite shades of Hemingway!

A fiercely independent city, Nîmes defied Parisian control for centuries, supporting the Huguenots in the 16thC and the local Camisards in the 17thC. Now it is a large, bustling, commercial city with a lively cultural life, including an opera, nine theatres or café-théatres, four good museums and an interesting town centre (see **NÎMES-WALK**). Nîmes also hosts the International Jazz Festival in July, an International Folklore Festival in July and August, and outdoor concerts in the Jardin de la Fontaine. It is a good centre for excursions southwest to Montpellier, southeast to the Camargue and Arles, east to Beaucaire, Tarascon and Avignon, and to the Pont du Gard and the *vin rosé* villages of Tavel and Lirac. The Tourist Office produces an excellent brochure, *What, Where, When and How in Nîmes*. See **NÎMES**, **Events**, **Tourist Information**.

Nostradamus, Michel de (1503-66): He was born at St. Rémy-de-Provence and became a famous physician, astrologer and prophet. In 1555 he produced his controversial book of predictions entitled *Centuries,* written in verse quatrains. The Musée de Nostradamus in Salon-de-Provence is located in the house where he spent the last 19 years of his life. Nearby is the 14thC Église de St. Laurent where he is buried. See **AIX-EN-PROVENCE-EXCURSION 1**.

Opening Times:
Banks – 0900-1200, 1400-1630 Mon.-Fri. (busy central branches stay open at lunchtime).
Bureau de change – vary from 0830/0900/0930-1800/2200 Mon.-Sat.
Churches – Main churches 0800-1600, i.e. from first Mass of the day until the last. Usually closed 1200-1400 in suburbs and villages.
Chemists – 0830-1200, 1400-1800 Mon.-Sat. (a Sun. roster usually operates).
Offices – 0830-1200, 1400-1800 Mon.-Sat.
Post Offices – 0800-1900 Mon.-Fri., 0800-1200 Sat.
Restaurants – Usually 1200-1400, 1900-2200. Many close on Mon., and some close for August and a winter month.
Shops – Vary enormously between 0800-1900, but smaller shops close for lunch between 1200-1400. Most food stores are closed on Mon., but remain open on Sun. am.

Orange: Pop: 28,000. In 36 BC the Romans settled veterans of Augustus's Second Legion in the old Celtic capital of Arausio. It became a bishopric in the 4thC with a population four times greater than today's. The Romans built temples, baths, a huge theatre, circus, amphitheatre,

triumphal arch, and a gymnasium and stadium 300 m long! Unfortunately, in 1622 Prince Maurice of Nassau decided to build a strong castle on the Capitol hill, and used most of the surviving Roman buildings as a stone quarry. However, the complex of the theatre, temple and gymnasium and stadium largely survived, as does the proud, lonely Arc de Triomphe (the third largest extant Roman triumphal arch in the world) at the north end of the town where the busy N 7 to Valence flows round it.

Annexed by the Papacy in 1274, Orange became a small principality, an enclave within the Comtat Venaissin (see **A-Z**) with Carpentras and Valréas, and did not rejoin France until 1713 under the Treaty of Utrecht. It is curious to recall that, technically, this little town belonged to England between 1689 and 1702 because, in 1689, William and

Mary of the House of Orange became British sovereigns! With its avenues of shady plane trees and narrow streets, Orange is proud of the magnificent Roman remains and plays host each summer to the Chorégies, a series of celebrated choral and opera productions attracting an international audience, which take place in the Roman theatre. Orange is also a good centre for excursions to Vaison-la-Romaine and the wine-growing areas. For restaurants try the moderately-priced Le Bec Fin, 14 rue Segond-Weber opposite the theatre and sample the *coq au vin de Châteauneuf-du-Pape* or *lapereau aux trois moutardes*. See ORANGE, **Events**, **Music**, **Tourist Information**.

Orientation: In large towns such as Marseille, Nîmes and Aix-en-Provence it is advisable to obtain a street map with index, usually free from the tourist office, to help you find your way around. In smaller towns such as Avignon, Arles and Orange the main attractions are usually to be found in the town centre and are easily accessible.

Palais des Papes: The huge, honey-coloured fortified palace built in the 14thC for the Papacy in Avignon. This is one of the major sights in Provence. See AVIGNON-WALK, WHAT TO SEE, **Papacy at Avignon**.

Papacy at Avignon: The Italians called it the 'Babylonian Captivity' and the theologians the 'Great Schism' – the period from 1307 until 1403 when the papacy was transferred from Rome to Avignon by French Popes. Pope Clement V, elected in 1305, moved initially to Carpentras, then to Avignon where Pope Benedict XII built the formidable gold-stone 'Old Palace'. Twenty years later Pope Clement VI created the equally splendid 'New Palace' and 82 cardinals built sumptuous quarters for themselves. Altogether seven French Popes ruled in Avignon, producing an admirable creative atmosphere for painters, musicians, poets and architects, and rich pickings for the court suppliers. From 1377-1403 corruption in Avignon matched the previous venality of Rome, and two rival papacies competed with each other – the French anti-Popes and a revived line of Italian Popes. The Great Schism eventually ended in 1449 and Avignon's glory immediately faded. See AVIGNON-WALK, WHAT TO SEE, **Palais des Papes**.

Jardin de la Fontaine

Parking: See **Driving**.

Parks & Gardens: In midsummer the public gardens provide a welcome break from sightseeing and the chance to relax in the shade. Marseille has the Jardin du Pharo, Jardin Colline Puget, Parc du Château Borély and Parc Balneaire du Prado, and finally the Jardin Valmer in the southern suburbs not too far from the Corniche. Aix-en-Provence has the Parc Jourdan, Parc Rambot, Jardin Vendôme and the park around the Musée Vasarély. In Avignon there is the Jardin du Rocher des Doms, and another garden in Pl. Perdiguier, near the Tourist Office. Arles has the Jardin d'Hiver, and Place Lamartine, while in Nîmes there is the lovely Jardin de la Fontaine and Esplanade de Gen. de Gaulle.

Passports & Customs: A passport from Britain, Ireland or other EC countries allows a 90-day stay with no visa required. Also acceptable are British visitors' passports and excursion passes (available from post offices). If you wish to stay for more than 90 days contact the local French police station (*commissariat de police*) or Service des Étrangers in Marseille at rue du C.-Becker, 2e, tel: 91919040, and in Nîmes at Ave Feuchères, tel: 66679691. Citizens from other countries, including the USA, Canada, Australia and New Zealand, require a visa which is easily obtained from French embassies and consulates in those countries. See **Customs Allowances**.

Petrarch, Francisco (1304-74): Francisco Petrarch, the Italian lyric poet, moved as a child with his family to the Papal court at Avignon in 1312. He saw (but did not speak to) a local married lady in church one day in April 1327. Inspired by pure love for her and disgusted by the corrupt court, he moved to the Abbaye de Sénanque and spent the years 1337 to 1353 at the nearby Fontaine-de-Vaucluse (see **A-Z**). There he wrote the 366 poems and sonnets of the *Canzonière* to the lady he called 'Laura'. See **AVIGNON-EXCURSION 1, MONASTERIES, ORANGE-EXCURSION 1**.

Petrol: Petrol (*l'essence*) is sold by the litre and prices are clearly marked in the petrol stations, which are usually self-service. There are petrol stations at frequent intervals along all the major roads and at the entry and exit points of all towns in Provence. Stations are usually open 0800-1900, but the Shell stations in Marseille (Bd des Dames) and Avignon (Bd Michel) are open 24 hr. Most petrol stations sell unleaded petrol. See **Driving**.

Picasso, Pablo (1881-1973): The brilliant Spanish painter and sculptor spent most of his early creative life in Paris, but settled in the French Riviera and Provence in 1945. In Antibes, during the period 1946-47, he set up a pottery centre at Vallauris (northeast of Cannes). In 1958 he purchased the chateau at Vauvenargues 14 km east of Aix-en-Provence (see **AIX-EN-PROVENCE-EXCURSION 2**) where he is buried. Much of his later work was done in Mougins, near Cannes, and the two major Picasso museums are in Antibes and in Vallauris. He presented the Musée Réattu in Arles (see **ARLES-WHAT TO SEE 1**) with 57 of his drawings, and the museum in Bollène, 23 km north of Orange also has an interesting collection of his work.

Pilgrimages: Several towns have annual pilgrimages:
Graveson (see **AVIGNON-EXCURSION 2**): *27 April;* Les Saintes-Maries-de-la-Mer: *24-25 May, Sun. nearest 22 October;* Marseille: *28 May, 14-15 August, 8 September;* Notre-Dame-de-Lumière, St. Etienne-du-Gres: *end of May;* Boulbon: *1 June;* Cuges-les-Pins: *13 June;* Allauch: *8 September.*

Police: They can be recognized by their dark blue uniforms and flat caps. Always address them as *Monsieur* (or *Madame*) *l'Agent*. They are usually helpful to tourists. Any theft or other incident should be reported to the nearest police station (*commissariat de police*).

Marseille	2 rue C.-Becker, 2e	tel: 91919040.
Nîmes		tel: 66679691.
Avignon		tel: 90851717.
Arles	Bd des Lices	tel: 90939834.
Aix		tel: 42260481.
Orange	Pl. Clemenceau	tel: 90517795.
Les Saintes-Maries-de-la-Mer		tel: 90478004.

See **Crime & Theft**, **Emergency Numbers**.

Pont du Gard: The most impressive Roman aqueduct in the world. It is situated between Avignon and Nîmes, 24 km from both. Built by the Emperor Agrippa in 19 BC to take water from Uzès to Nîmes, it has three tiers of arches spanning the River Gardon. See **NÎMES-EXCURSION**.

Post Offices: Look for the yellow signs marked PTT or POSTES (post boxes are the same colour). They provide full postal services, including telephones for both local and long-distance calls. Phones are metered and the call can be paid for when you are finished. In addition a currency exchange service is often available. Postage stamps can also be purchased from *tabacs*.
Main post offices:

Marseille	1 Pl. Hôtel des Postes, tel: 91903133.
Nîmes	Bd Gambetta, tel: 66672745.
Avignon	Ave du President Kennedy, tel: 90867800.
Arles	5 Bd des Lices.
Aix	2 rue Lapierre, tel: 42276800.

See **Opening Times**, **Telephones & Telegrams**.

Public Holidays: 1 Jan. (New Year's Day); Easter Monday; 1 May (Labour Day); 8 May; Ascension Day (40 days after Easter); Whit. Monday; 14 July; 15 Aug. (Assumption); 11 Nov.; 25 Dec. (Christmas Day). Banks close at noon on the nearest working day before a public holiday.

Rabies: Still exists in Provence as in other parts of the Continent. As a precaution have all animal bites treated immediately by a doctor.

Railways:
SNCF stations:

Marseille	Gare St. Charles, Ave Pierre Semard, tel: 91085050.
Nîmes	Ave Feuchères, tel: 66235050.
Avignon	Porte de la République, tel: 90825629.
Arles	Ave Tallabot, tel: 90963625.
Aix	Ave Victor Hugo, tel: 42275163.
Orange	Ave Frédéric Mistral, tel: 90341782.

Marseille is the main railway terminus. Trains run to Aix hourly: journey time 35 min, 30F; Arles every 30 min: journey time1 hr, 60F; Avignon every 30 min, journey time 1 hr, 75F; Nîmes hourly, journey time 75 min, 50F; Cassis every 30 min, journey time 20 min, 25F. Stations have all the usual services, including currency exchange, left

luggage facilities and Tourist Information, and often a bicycle rental office. Remember to validate your rail ticket in the orange ticket punch at the entrance to the platform (*composter votre billet*). See **Transport**.

Religious Services: France is predominantly a Roman Catholic country, but churches of every denomination can be found in Provence. Below is a list of Protestant churches:

Marseille Culte Protestante, consistoire 15 rue Grignan, 6e.
Culte Anglican, 4 rue de Belloi, 6e.
Nîmes Église Reformée, 3 rue Claude Brousson.
Aix Église Anglicane, 7 cours de la Trinité.
Église Reformée de France, 4 rue Villars.

Consult the local Tourist Office for times of services. See **Synagogues**, **Tourist Information**.

René of Anjou, 'Good King' (1409-80): A talented, popular Count of Provence. He was a scholar, poet, musician and mathematician, who, by his wise rule, brought a golden era of romance and prosperity to Provence. His court was in Aix-en-Provence and his castle at Tarascon. See CHATEAUX, **Troubadours**.

River Rhône: This is the longest river in France and forms the boundary between Provence, on the east, and Languedoc, on the west. The Greeks and Romans sailed up the wide river trading wine and foodstuffs and protected the river's harbours with castles and small fortified towns. From the 13thC Beaucaire, opposite Tarascon, hosted the greatest medieval trading fair in Provence, and perhaps in all of France. In July of each year 300,000 people came from all over Europe and up to 500 ships berthed on the west side of the Rhône (see ARLES-EXCURSION). The Romans had built a wooden bridge at Arles, and in the 12thC the river was also bridged at Avignon (St. Bénézet) (see AVIGNON-WHAT TO SEE). Another bridge was built further north at Pont St. Esprit in the 13thC. For another six centuries the river remained the lifeline of Provence, and British travellers on the Grand Tour wrote feelingly of the boat trip south from Lyons to Avignon. The railways, which appeared in the mid-19thC, killed off the river trade and traffic. Since

Aix-en-Provence

1934 no less than 23 hydro-electric stations and dams, although blocking the river, have created cheap electricity for the region. Just as importantly, irrigation canals have kept the market gardens prosperous around Cavaillon (see **AVIGNON-EXCURSION 1**) and Carpentras (see **ORANGE-EXCURSION 1**), and the fruit orchards, vineyards and olive groves fertile and luxuriant. See **Boat Trips**.

Roman Sites:

Excavated towns	Vaison-la-Romaine (see ORANGE-EXCURSION 1)
	St. Rémy-de-Provence (see ARLES-EXCURSION)
Theatres	Orange (see ORANGE-WHAT TO SEE)
	Arles (see ARLES-WHAT TO SEE 1, **Arles**)
	Vaison-la-Romaine (see ORANGE-EXCURSION 1)
Amphitheatres	Nîmes (see NÎMES-WHAT TO SEE 1)
	Arles (see ARLES-WHAT TO SEE 1, **Arles**).
Arches	St. Rémy-de-Provence (see ARLES-EXCURSION)
	Orange (see ORANGE-WHAT TO SEE)
Temples	Nîmes (Maison Carrée) (see NÎMES-WHAT TO SEE)
Aqueducts	Pont du Gard (see NÎMES-EXCURSION)
	Barbegal, near Arles.

St. Rémy-de-Provence: Pop: 9000. A small town 23 km from both Avignon and Arles, noted for the Roman town of Glanum and the Les Antiques memorials by the roadside 1 km south. See ARLES-EXCURSION, **Roman Sites.**

Salins du Midi: Located to the west of the Camargue around Aigues-Mortes, the Salins du Midi produce nearly 600,000 tonnes of salt from local salt marshes each year. The paddy fields are flooded with saltwater between March and September to a depth of one foot and the salt crystals are dried out in huge white glittering piles, called *camelles*, up to 20 m high. In the 13thC monks washed, dried and crushed salt crystals for sale. Visits can be arranged by the Tourist Office in July and August. See **Camargue**.

Santons: Clay figures of 'little saints' painted in bright colours have been a favourite craft-toy in the region for two centuries. A collection may run to 40 different figures; the Holy Family, shepherds, the Three Kings, etc. See AIX-EN-PROVENCE-MUSEUMS 1, MARSEILLE-WALK, **Best Buys**.

Shopping: Ideas for souvenirs or presents from Provence include wine, *pastis*, herbs, olives, olive oil, truffles, lavender, local honey and confectionery.

Santon

English Bookshops:

Marseille	Diffusion Générale de Librairie, 21 rue Paradis.
Nîmes	Librairie Anglaise, 8 rue Dorée.
Aix	Paradox, 2 rue Reine-Jeanne.

See **Best Buys**, **Wines**.

Smoking: Smoking is not permitted in churches, museums, art galleries and theatres, and is discouraged in restaurants. Trains have separate non-smoking compartments.

Sports: All water sports are available, with 15 marinas along the Mediterranean coast of Provence providing sailing, windsurfing, swimming, fishing and canoeing. Most villages and many camp sites have tennis courts and a swimming pool (*piscine*). Riding is very popular, and there are over 30 *centres equestres*, mainly in the Vaucluse department and the Camargue. There are eight golf clubs, 10 flying clubs, rock/hill-climbing clubs and caving/pot-holing clubs, mainly in the Vaucluse. Specialist sports include archery, hang-gliding, rifle range shooting and snow skiing (in the mountain ranges of the Vaucluse). Spectator sports, including football, rugby, horse riding, motocross and cycle racing can all be seen in the appropriate season. Horse racing takes place in Marseille at Parc Borély, Promenade de la Plage, 8e.

For details of sports, whether participatory or as a spectator, contact the local Tourist Office.

Synagogues: The synagogues in Avignon, Carpentras (1367), Cavaillon (1772) (see **AVIGNON-EXCURSION 1**) and L'Isle-sur-la-Sorgue have offered sanctuary to the Jewish community for centuries. Indeed, the synagogue in Carpentras is the oldest in France (see **ORANGE-EXCURSION 1**).

Taxis: It is easy to obtain a taxi in the major towns in Provence. You can either pick one up at the numerous taxi ranks or order one by telephone.

Marseille	Maison du Taxi, tel: 91959250.
	Marseille Taxi, tel: 91022020.
Nîmes	Taxis Radio Artisans Nîmois, tel: 66294011/66294349.
Avignon	Radio Taxi, tel: 90822020.
Aix	Taxi Radio Aixois, tel: 42277111 (day), 42262930 (night).

Taxi ranks can be found at SNCF stations. See **Tipping**.

Fabrique
PATISSIER

Calissons
ARD
d'Aix CONFISEUR

Telephones & Telegrams: You will find numerous pay-phones but the majority require a phonecard rather than coins. Coin-operated phones take 1F, 5F and 10F coins. Phonecards (*télécartes*) are available from post offices and *tabacs* and cost 50F and 100F. To use a card phone, lift the receiver, insert the card, pull down the handle above it and dial. For coin-operated telephones, insert the money first, then dial. In post offices (see **A-Z**) you can use a metered telephone which lets you make the call before paying. If using a café telephone you may have to buy a token (*jeton*) at the bar. Calls from your hotel room will be subject to a hefty surcharge. Cheap rates operate 2130-0800 Mon.-Fri., after 1400 Sat. and all day Sun. and public holidays. To telephone the UK from France, dial 19, wait for the tone to change, dial 44 (11 for the USA, 61 for Australia) then the STD number minus the first 0, then the number. To telephone France from the UK, dial 01033 then the eight-figure provincial number. You can receive return calls at telephone booths. Telegrams can be sent from a post office or over the telephone by dialling 001111.

Television & Radio: There are six channels on French TV: TF1, A2, FR3, LA5, M6 and Canal+ (the first paying and coded network). News broadcasts are at 0800, 1300, 2000 and 2300.
It is possible to receive BBC Radio 4 by tuning in to 1500 m on long wave, and the BBC World Service is on 463 m medium wave.

Time Difference: French standard time is GMT plus one hour and the clocks go forward an hour in summer. France is thus always one hour ahead of Britain.

Tipping: A 15% service charge is included in your bill at all hotels and restaurants, as is TVA (VAT), so there is no need to leave a tip unless you feel the service has been particularly good. If you pay by cash, any small change is usually left for the waiter. Hotel

porters expect to receive 10F per item of luggage, chambermaids 10F per day, taxi drivers 10-15% of the fare and hairdressers about 10F.

Toilets: Public toilets are usually situated in public parks, town squares, and in bus and railway stations. Hygiene standards have improved, but toilets in cafés and bars are not always *comme il faut.* Men's stand-up, green-painted, iron-clad urinals are giving way to smart coin-operated unisex *cabines,* which usually cost 2F.

Tourist Information: The Tourist Offices in Provence stock a wide range of leaflets, maps, tours and advice. The staff are usually very helpful but rarely speak English.

Marseille	4 La Canebière 13001, tel: 91549111 (close to Vieux Port), Gare St. Charles, tel: 91505918.
Nîmes	6 rue Auguste, 30000 (near Maison Carrée), tel: 66672911.
Avignon	41 cours Jean Jaurès, 84000, tel: 90826511.
Arles	Esplanade Charles-de-Gaulle, 13200 (off Bd des Lices), tel: 90962935.
Aix	Pl. du General-de-Gaulle, 13100, tel: 42260293.
Orange	cours Aristide Briande, 84100 (west on the D 17), tel: 90347088.
Uzès	Ave de la Libération, tel: 66226888.

Offices are usually open 0900-1800 Mon.-Fri., 0900-1200, 1400-1800 Sat. but are closed on Sun. except during festivals. Some charge 10F for making hotel reservations. See **Accommodation**, **Tours**, **What's On**.

Tours: Most Tourist Offices in Provence offer guided town walks for a fee, and will give advice and make reservations for coach tours to the neighbouring countryside attractions. Enquiries and bookings can also be made at the SNCF station, *gare routière* (bus station) and a range of travel agents. See **Tourist Information**.

Transport: Provence has several airports, a good network of *autoroutes,* local roads, and good train and bus services. There is a Métro system in Marseille. See **Airports**, **Boat Trips**, **Buses**, **Métro**, **Railways**, **Taxis**.

Traveller's Cheques: See **Money**.

Troubadours: During the 11th-13thC romantic 'Courts of Love' flourished in the south of France. Poetic young courtiers composed, and wandering minstrels performed, love songs and ballads in praise of the noble (married) ladies. In Provence the two key periods of chivalric lyric verse were centred on the warrior lords in the hilltop fortress and town of Les Baux (a line which died out in the late 14thC) (see **ARLES-EXCURSION**), and on the courts of Aix-en-Provence in the 12th-15thC, particularly under the inspired, civilized King René of Anjou, Count of Provence (see **René of Anjou**).

Vaison-la-Romaine: Pop: 6000. 27 km northeast of Orange. This is an interesting small town bisected by the River Ouvèze, with Roman town excavations on the north bank and a medieval hill town on the south bank. See **ORANGE-EXCURSION 1**.

Van Gogh, Vincent (1853-90): The great Impressionist painter was born in Brabant, but spent the last two years of his life in Provence, initially in Arles, but after cutting off part of his ear, he moved voluntarily to a mental asylum in St. Rémy-de-Provence (see **ARLES-EXCURSION**). This brilliant, passionate painter created colourful masterpieces of local people and places. During the last 15 months of his life he painted 300 canvases – half his entire output. In Arles he painted the Café du Soir, the Café du Nuit, the Yellow House, the sad, gloomy Alyscamps (see **ARLES-WHAT TO SEE 2**), the drawbridge of Langlois, the cornfields at sunset and of course the beautiful, golden sunflowers. He spent a week at Les Saintes-Maries-de-la-Mer and there painted *A View of La Crau* and *Fishing Boats on the Beach*. Finally admitted to the St. Rémy-de-Provence asylum, he finished his life with a flurry of masterpieces and then shot himself, aged 37. His last written words to his brother were, 'Misery will never end'. His paintings now command millions of pounds at international auctions.

What's On: Most Tourist Offices publish a monthly news magazine or leaflet with listings of current events and entertainments, such as the

monthly magazines *Nouvelles de Marseille, Le Mois à Aix, A comme Avignon* and *Avignon Pratique*. Every town and village has a series of events variously described as *fête votive* (after the patron saint), *spectacle, manifestation* or *animation*. A *foire* or fair will have a band, some dancing in the evening, roundabouts and many *artisanal* stalls selling pottery, glassware, leather work and local food delicacies. Ask for details from the local Tourist Office. See **Events**, **Music Festivals**, **Tourist Information**.

Wines: The Greeks first brought the vine to Provence 2500 years ago, and vine-growing intensified under the Romans. Over 130,000 ha are currently under production and some of the locally-produced red wines (Châteauneuf-du-Pape, Gigondas) and *vins rosé* (Tavel) have an international reputation. Visitors interested in wine should base themselves in Orange or Avignon. Some of the lesser-known wines deserve to be tried, and a visit to one of the local wine co-operatives allows you to taste a wide range of varieties before buying, perhaps, a mixed case. When in Aix-en-Provence make a point of trying locally grown Palette wines (*rosé*); in Cassis try the dry, pale yellow white wine; in Nîmes ask for Lirac *rosé* as an alternative to Tavel; in Avignon try Vacqueyras as an alternative to Châteauneuf-du-Pape and Gigondas; in Orange or Vaison-la-Romaine try Rasteau, fortified deep gold or tawny wines; and in Carpentras try Beaumes-de-Venise, the pale golden fortified muscat wine. Generic wines include the well-known Côtes du Rhône and Côtes du Rhône Villages, and the less well-known Côtes du Lubéron and Côtes du Ventoux. A visit to Provence is an excellent opportunity to try some new wines, which are usually quite inexpensive. See **ORANGE-EXCURSIONS 1 & 2, Wine Tours**.

Wine Tours: The best centres for regional wine tours are: Avignon, to see the vineyards of Châteauneuf-du-Pape, Tavel and Lirac; and Orange, to see all of the above plus the vineyards of Gigondas, Vacqueyras and Beaumes-de-Venise. The wines of the Côteaux d'Aix and Palette can be tasted on tours from Aix-en-Provence and the wines of Cassis on tours from Marseille. See **Wines**.

Youth Hostels: The YHA in France is known as the Auberges de Jeunesse. The hostels provide cheap accommodation but you must be aged between 13-18. You are allowed to stay for a maximum of five consecutive nights in any one hostel.
Marseille – Auberge de Jeunesse de Bois-Luzy, 76 Ave de Bois-Luzy, 13012, tel: 91490818; Auberge de Jeunesse de Bonneveine, 47 Ave Joseph-Vidal, 13008, tel: 91732181.
Nîmes – Auberge de Jeunesse (IYHF), chemin de l'Auberge de Jeunesse, tel: 66232504.
Avignon – Foyer YMCA, 7 bis Bd de la Justice, tel: 90254620.
Arles – Auberge de Jeunesse (ALAJ), Ave Maréchal Foch, tel: 90961825.
Aix – Auberge de Jeunesse (IYHF), 3 Ave Marcel Pagnol, tel: 42201599.
Les Saintes-Maries-de-La-Mer – Auberge de Jeunesse (IYHF), Ave Pioch Badet, tel: 90979172.
Tarascon – Auberge de Jeunesse, 31 Bd Gambetta, tel: 90910408.
There are other youth hostels in Séguret, tel: 90469331, and Fontaine-de-Vaucluse, tel: 90203165. Some cities also have a Centre d'Information Jeunesse which offers comprehensive advice on youth activities and sports. These can be found in Marseille at 4 rue de la Visitation, tel: 91499155, and in Aix-en-Provence at 37 bis Bd Aristide Briand, tel: 42960376.

The publishers welcome corrections and suggestions from readers; write to:
The Publishing Manager, Travel Guides, HarperCollins Publishers, PO Box, Glasgow G4 ONB

La Rotonde